The *Crooked* Pitch

The Curveball in American Baseball History

ALGONQUIN BOOKS OF CHAPEL HILL · 1988

The *Crooked* Pitch

The Curveball in American Baseball History

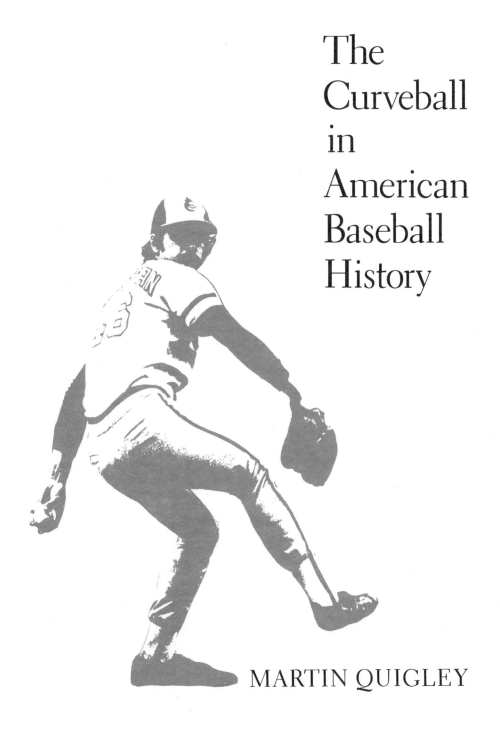

MARTIN QUIGLEY

ALGONQUIN BOOKS OF CHAPEL HILL
Post Office Box 2225
Chapel Hill, North Carolina 27515-2225

in association with
Taylor Publishing Company
1550 West Mockingbird Lane
Dallas, Texas 75235

LIBRARY OF CONGRESS CATALOGING-IN-PUBLICATION DATA
Quigley, Martin Peter, 1913–
    The crooked pitch: the curveball in American baseball history/Martin Quigley.

    p.   cm.
    Includes index.
    ISBN 0-912697-82-2 (pbk.)
    1. Pitching (Baseball)   2. Baseball—United States—
History.   I. Title.
GV871.Q54   1988
796.357'22—DC19   87-23168
                    CIP

*This book was written with the help and wisdom of
Paul Mac Farlane, director of historical research and
archivist for* The Sporting News. *For the courtesies of the
management and staff of* TSN, *and for the stories of
many of the players and reporters famous and obscure
that live again in these pages, the author expresses his
thanks.*

CONTENTS

LIST OF ILLUSTRATIONS

FOUNDING FATHERS

Alexander Cartwright,
who established the
dimensions of the diamond.
The Sporting News

Henry Chadwick,
whose rule change
made the curveball possible.
The Sporting News

Major-General Abner
Doubleday, who
allegedly invented the
game of baseball at
Cooperstown, N.Y., in
1839. *The Sporting News*

Albert G. Spalding,
who saw to it that
baseball was officially
the "invention of a red-
blooded American."
The Sporting News

PREFACE TO THE PAPERBACK EDITION

In researching and writing this definitive account of the curveball in American baseball history, I had the help and wisdom of Paul Mac Farlane, the historian of *The Sporting News*, with headquarters a few minutes down the road from my home in St. Louis. Thanks to Richard Waters, president and chief executive officer, I was permitted access to the baseball fact and lore accumulated and preserved by *The Sporting News* in its century of unparalleled informational services and leadership in professional sports.

When the first hardcover edition of *The Crooked Pitch* was published, the experts of the baseball world, which includes the millions of its fans, were looking forward with inevitably myopic vision to their expectancies of individual and team performances in the 1984 season. As this paperback edition goes to market, we are at it again—on the clean slate of the 1988 season. But again, the only certainty is that there will be more unpredicted surprises and unpredictable happenstances than fulfilled expectancies. Thus it has been and thus, because of the myriad vagaries inherent in the game, it will always be.

During these four years I have been looking expectantly for errors of fact or significant omission that seemed inevitable in the research and writing of so complex, controversial, and vital a part of the development of baseball into our National Pastime. With Mac's help, I checked out every suggestion of error of fact—and found none! The historical facts, the aerodynamic principles, and the achievements of the practitioners of the curveball stand as written.

A good many major leaguers have read and commented on the authenticity of their records, techniques, and anecdotal lore as reported here. Not one scored any fact an error. Two of the greatest of the great who ever pitched or batted—Bob Feller and Ted Williams—said they could not find a single error in curves as thrown or in curves to try to hit.

Two opinionated predictions I made, though, have not come to pass. One was that the exact number of hits credited to Ty Cobb would be a matter of dispute as Pete Rose inexorably approached his career record. But Paul Mac Farlane's impeccable research placed Ty's record total at 4,190. Then Pete made the question academic by breezing way past any claim in 1985. At the end of the 1986 season, probably his last as a player, he had set a new record, not likely to be approached by any existing or unborn player, of 4,256 hits in his twenty-four-year career as a major league batter.

When, in the 1982 season, both Nolan Ryan and Steve Carlton passed Walter Johnson's career record of 3,508 strikeouts, I thought it reasonable to suppose that Steve's slider would be more effectively durable than Nolan's fastball in the waning years of their careers. Not so. At the end of the 1986 season, Steve had struck out 4,040 batters, while Nolan's record of 4,277 was still upward bound. It seems certain that no one but Nolan will break his present record—just as nobody, within imaginable changes in the game, has a shot at topping his record of five no-hitters.

Anyway, here it comes again. Take your cuts at it. Watch out for that crooked pitch!

St. Louis, Missouri   MARTIN QUIGLEY
June 30, 1987

Arthur (Candy) Cummings, the man who invented the curveball.

The Joys of Deception

Candy Cummings is enshrined in baseball's Hall of Fame as the originator of the curveball. If as a kid I had known about him, he, and not the fictional Baby Elton, would have been my hero and inspiration.

Baby was the diminutive protagonist of one of the many stories by Ralph Henry Barbour about athletes of diamond, gridiron, and track in the prep schools of the East, around and just after the turn of the twentieth century. An athlete and coach himself (he wrote a book about how to instruct and coach young baseball players), Barbour was a fine storyteller, with a narrative pace that kept several generations of boys enthralled with the pressure performances of his heroes at the marvelous moment of climax, and, of course, victory in games and footraces. Though when I read them his stories were somewhat out of date—a touchdown counted only five points and the extra point had to be tried from where the goal line was crossed—they were still in and out of the public libraries on a weekly basis in the mid-1920s.

Baby Elton was my hero because, like me, he was a wiry shrimp who depended upon quickness, determination, and deception to survive and win. I admired and envied the heroes of prodigious strength like Center Rush Rowland, but I could feel that I was in Baby's cleats and spikes. In the championship football game, Baby, as quarterback, sent the entire momentum of his team to the right while he kept the ball and scampered across the goal line with the winning touchdown, untouched by the deceived defenders.

In the championship baseball game, with his team trying to hold its one-run lead, he was called to the mound in the ninth inning to relieve the exhausted starting pitcher. The bases were loaded, with two out and a 3–2 count on the mighty clean-up batter. Baby knew that this was the moment to throw the outdrop curve he had practiced for many a lonely hour. He felt for the high seams, gripped the ball, wound up as the runners took off, and aimed it at the batter's head. Seeing that the ball would hit him, the courageous batter "stood like a Trojan" to take his lumps for his team. But, obedient to the spinning charm Baby had put on it, the ball curved sharply down and across the plate for the third strike.

Inspired, I went to work learning and practicing to throw curves. In addition to a fairly strong and tireless arm, I had an innate inquisitiveness about what a baseball could be made to do. With occasional instruction on mechanics from the grown-up pitchers on the industrial and town ball teams I served as batboy, and with persistent practice in sandlot games with my peers, I learned with increasing success to throw inshoot and upshoot fastballs, the underhanded rainbow drop fastball, the underhanded curve, the sidearm curve, the three-quarter-arm outdrop, the overhanded drop, and the screwball, as the pitches were called in those days. My efforts to achieve a spinless knuckler and a palm ball blooper were thwarted because of a lack of consistent control. I could control an overhanded forkball that came in like a fastball and arched down at the plate, but I did not have the velocity to give it a sharp break—until I learned to stick a phonograph needle in the seam. The main trouble I had in trying to throw spitters and their vaseline variants was that most of my playing was done in two-ball leagues; you need a new ball with smooth surfaces to throw those devils.

Scuffling around in the Depression, and later while doing my bit in the Air Force, I played in town leagues, industrial leagues, in the Civilian Conservation Corps, and at the military bases where time and chance took me. When, after bumming around with construction laborers and itinerant athletes for three years after high school, I got to college, I concentrated on books and girls instead of baseball and went forth from the University of Minnesota with a good craft, journalism, and a wonderful wife, Margaret, both of which I still have.

More than anything else, it was the phonograph needle pitch that fulfilled my love of deception and made me a reliable relief pitcher. I learned it in the CCC at Fort Ripley, Minnesota, where our manual labor at $30 a month turned a place of old gravel pits and scrub woodland into the lovely state park it is today. A stringbean of a pitcher called Stork, who was on parole from doing five-to-forty years in the so-called reformatory at St. Cloud for burglary, taught me the magic of the pitch. Out of the hundred city guys and country boys in the barracks, we shaped up the inevitable baseball team, and on Sunday afternoons played the tough town teams for fifty miles around. It took Stork at his best, with me in occasional relief, to hang in against them.

On one occasion, we had the Fourth of July doubleheader coming up against Sleepy Eye, the toughest team around. A week ahead, our skipper and catcher, Joe, decided our best chance was to start me in the first game, hoping I could keep the score close for five or six innings, and then bring in Stork to nail it down and, without cooling off, pitch the second game. Stork, figuring I would need "something extra," especially against their lefthanded power hitters, taught me the phonograph needle pitch that he had learned on the stir team from a safecracker who had learned it from his Uncle Fred, pitching coach for the Minneapolis Millers.

With a pack (fifty for a dime) of old-fashioned 78 RPM phonograph needles in our back pockets, Stork showed me how he would fish one between his fingers from a natural hands-on-hips stance and, while looking in for the sign, press it firmly against his belt buckle into the seam. The weight of the needle made the spinning ball perform predictable tricks. A fastballing lefthander who came over the top, Stork would use it only a dozen or so times a game, to give extra rising zip to his fastball and six inches more break to his nickel curve. Pitching to our teammates every evening that week, we found that the needle had negligible effect on my low-velocity fastball and too much on my high-rotation sidearm curve, but it made a crazy sinker out of my forkball and a wide curve out of my screwball. The beauty was that the needle would pop out of the seam on contact with the catcher's mitt or when hit, and there was no detectable trace of illegality on the ball. (Neither umpires nor opposing teams were equipped with metal detectors.) My problem was loading the needle without getting caught. It was one thing for Stork to fish out a needle with his long lock-picking fingers, and another for me with my honest, nervous paw. I solved it by sticking a dozen needles in the right seam of my pants, from which I could pluck them with a natural hand-rubbing move, and by scattering others near the resin bag in the grass behind the mound.

As it happened, we jumped off with three runs in the first inning and four more in the third, so I could have had a cakewalk with my regular junk, but I used about thirty needles just for the fun of it, and breezed through the full game. The ball behaved unbelievably. On at least seven different occasions that day, the umpire called for the ball, examined it, and each time gave it back, shaking his head.

My fascination with the curveball, both the honest variety and its crooked cousins, has continued through my many years as a baseball fan, into my senility as a softball pitcher for a team of youngsters in their twenties.

Like Baby Elton and me, Candy Cummings was a shrimp who could not get by on his beef. He was 5'4" and weighed but 92 pounds when, at age fourteen in 1862, he began trying to make a baseball curve. Unlike Baby, he was real. Unlike me, he went on to carve out a career as a major leaguer and on into the Hall of Fame.

Since Candy's time, the various curveballs and their deceptions have become the most important element in making baseball a fascinating game of uncertainties—our national pastime. The story of the curveball is the story of the game itself. Some would say of life itself.

Bobby Matthews, said to have been a practitioner of the spitball back in the 1880s. *The Sporting News*

Tony (The Count) Mullane could come in with a pitch either right- or lefthanded. *The Sporting News*

James (Deacon) White, early professional curveball virtuoso. *The Sporting News*

CHAPTER ONE

The Great Equalizer

"Oh, the joys and miseries it has caused!"

Thus spake Hub Kittle about the curveball. Through the six decades of his professional career, beginning in the 1930s and into the 1980s, the canny pitching coach of the St. Louis Cardinals in 1982–83 has thrown it and taught it for money. He has seen it as the difference between winning and losing many thousands of professional baseball games. He has seen it as the difference between great careers and no careers at all, between ends to careers and fifteen more years in the majors, as the difference in the direction of flow of millions of dollars, of sound sleep and a night (a lifetime) of "if I'da only. . . ." His utterance is an echo from a hundred years of baseball history before him, and in years to come will be sworn to as truth by players yet unborn.

The honest curveball and its crooked cousins are the most important equalizers of the magical differences, in inches and fractions of

7

inches and of seconds and milliseconds, between safe or out, win or lose. Without the deception of the curve, baseball would have become just another sport for young men of premium size and strength. Mastery of the curve—of one or more of its deceptive variants—gives heroic employment to small men, 200-plus wins for the great pitcher, and new life to old men in major league baseball. The curve makes baseball a game of first choices and second guesses—on the mound, at the plate, in the field, in the dugout and coaching boxes, and in the stands. It is the creator of abiding uncertainty, lasting until the final out of each game.

The curving ball—and the possibility that an apparently straight ball will suddenly change direction—makes successful batting the most difficult achievement in sports. To achieve precise contact with a proper point on a rounded bat upon the leading edge of a round ball that is spinning, curving, floating, or dancing plateward at a speed of from 35 MPH to 100 MPH, thrown from 60 feet away, takes both deliberate thought about and adjustment to what to expect, followed by a split-second decision on what to do once the pitcher has released the pitch of his choice. It takes better vision and more perfect coordination of muscles than any other skill in any sport. A batter who can do it three out of ten times at bat is a fixed star in baseball's firmament; one who does it four out of ten times for an entire season becomes an immortal in the game's pantheon of heroes.

In the confrontation between batter and pitcher, it is the curveball that makes the batter the underdog. This may be why, along with the fun of hits and runs, the greatest heroes among the fans are the most successful batters. In interviews with 194 random fans during the 1983 season, Bob McMahon of Media, Pennsylvania, found that among the interviewees' fifteen all-time favorites—Ruth, Mantle, Mays, Williams, DiMaggio, Musial, Clemente, Reggie Jackson, Gehrig, Rose, and Cobb—only one pitcher, Sandy Koufax, was included. He ranked ninth, after Clemente. Of those still playing, Rose was the big favorite—a tribute to his fearless determination to hit any damn pitch thrown (and, of course, his hustle and the defensive versatility that enables managers to keep his bat in the lineup somewhere).

The timing and path of the swing are the two most important factors in the batter's ability to hit the ball precisely. A millisecond too soon or too late is the difference between fair or foul. At 60 feet, a 100-mile-per-hour fastball travels from release to point of precise contact in .41 of a second, an 80-MPH curve in half a second, a 50-

MPH change-up in .82 of a second. A 35-MPH knuckler or blooper pitch gives the batter a full second to pick up the flight of the confounded thing, and to hold his swing until it arrives.

But it is trickier than that. While the slab on the mound is 60 feet, 6 inches from the plate, a pitched ball may be in the air for as little as 55 feet to as much as 62 feet, depending upon the pitcher's height, length of stride, and delivery motion, and upon how far up or back the batter is standing in his box. These variations make an enormous difference in split seconds. A 100-mile-per-hour fastball from 55 feet, for example, arrives at the point of contact .03 of a second sooner than one from 60 feet. These differences are in the pitcher's favor, because it is he who determines what the batter can only guess at— the speed and action of the ball.

Take a look, with the batter, at a 100-mile-per-hour fastball. It is coming at you at the rate of 15 feet every tenth of a second. During the first tenth of a second you must pick up its probable flight path and judge its velocity; in the second tenth, you must determine the likelihood of its coming into the strike zone and decide whether or not to swing, a decision which may depend upon the ball-and-strike count. All right, you're going to swing: In the third tenth of a second, taking the bat back to start your swing, you must judge where it will be in the strike zone a tenth of a second later when your swing intersects with its path, and not a millisecond too soon or too late to get a hit.

If the pitcher took a little off the pitch and it's an 85-MPH fastball that you otherwise judged correctly, you foul off the pitch. If the pitch comes in looking like a 100-MPH fastball (which can be curving down or sailing up) but is actually an 85-MPH sharp-breaking slider, you swing too soon at where it isn't. If you're poised for the fastball and the pitch is a leisurely sweeping curve of 75 MPH, you must break your swing to take a lunging poke at it as it breaks down, in, or away; your best hope is for contact that produces a lucky blooper hit or a chopped high bounder that if you are swift afoot you can beat to first base.

The extra decision time that the curveball gives makes some batters better curveball hitters than fastball hitters. But if they don't have the quickness and vision to hit the fastball, too, a steady diet of the latter soon shrinks their batting averages to the vanishing-from-the-major-leagues point.

Most good hitters, say in the .270 to .300 range (modern levels, of course), set themselves and wait for a particular pitch, a curve or fastball. After two strikes, however, they have got to guess at what's coming and hope they have guessed their timing right. Lonnie Smith, after a 1983 St. Louis Cardinal loss to Fernando Valenzuela of the Dodgers, lamented: "We waited for his screwball, and he threw the fastball past us." More generally, Bobby Murcer put it this way: "You decide you'll wait for your pitch. As the ball starts toward the plate, you think about your stance. And then you think about your swing. Then you realize that the ball that went by you for a strike was your pitch."

Some great hitters—Stan Musial, for example—always set themselves for the fastball, confident that they could instantly identify which pitch was coming and adjust their timing to meet it at the front door. An even greater hitter, Ted Williams, anticipated nothing, accepting whatever the pitcher decided to throw. He would pull the trigger on the fastball, or wait and wait and wait for a piece of junk to arrive and hit it on the nose. A spectacular example was his home run in the 1946 All-Star game off one of Rip Sewell's famously slow bloopers— his "eephus" pitch, Rip called it—that finally settled into the strike zone from an altitude of 25 feet.

Both Williams and Musial, and probably other Hall of Fame batters, had better than perfect (20/20) vision. One afternoon Ted, out with Paul Mac Farlane, pointed into the high sky and remarked, "That vulture is really way up there, isn't he?" In Paul's 20/20 vision there was no bird in the sky. In a few minutes, though, the vulture soared down into Paul's range of vision.

In 1962, the St. Louis Cardinals played their final spring game with their farm club in the old Houston ballpark. Next day, back home to open the season, the players complained that the lights were so bad they had trouble seeing the ball. I asked Stanley if they were really that bad. "Worse," he said. "I couldn't see which way the ball was spinning until it was halfway on me."

And there is "the melody of the sphere" (as someone described the sound of a Koufax curve), which may be an aid in tracking the flight of a ball in the air. Some otologists suggest the probability that the sound waves being emitted from a spinning ball help guide batters and outfielders on the dead run to the precise point of contact with it. While not conscious of sound, they may be responding to impulses received sooner through one ear than the other. While some human senses have been dulled by centuries of nonimportance to survival, they are never turned off completely; like sight and feel and taste, the hearing mechanism is more acute in some folks than in others. Musial said he "never heard a ball do a thing." Williams said the only sound he ever heard from a ball—and only rarely, in the deep silence of a tense moment—was the slight rasp of a pitcher's fingers coming off the seams at release. So . . .

A big factor in making the hitting of a baseball so difficult is fear. The uncertainty of the velocity and action and destination of a pitch is compounded by the aberrations of a pitcher's control, by the "purpose" pitch (high and tight to discourage aggressiveness at the plate), and by deliberate and vicious beanballs to make every batter afraid, or in any event, wary, of getting hit. A curveball aimed at a batter's head, but spun to break late down and away, may cause the batter to bail out on a strike pitch. I once asked the late Kenny Boyer about it. "Listen," he said, "there's fear in everybody's ass."

It is the curveball that makes the fastball effective. Without its surprise and deception, batters soon pick up the timing of a pitcher's fastball. Some pitchers with negligible fastballs achieve long and great careers with their curves and control. Walter Johnson is the only great pitcher who relied on smoke alone, as we shall see in a closer look at the fastball. Other pitchers with supreme fastballs either came in with curve variations or developed them to stay in the game. An example of one who did not is Paul Dean. The consensus of his peers is that if he had acquired a good curve, especially the slider, he would have been an invincible pitcher for many more years. (By the time Dizzy—"Me'n Paul will fog 'em past 'em"—pitched curves to stay on somebody's payroll, his arm was shot.)

An example of a fastballer whose career went into orbit after he blended more curves with his smoker is Bob Feller. Another is Lefty Grove. When, at seventeen, Feller broke in with Cleveland in 1936, he was a fastballer, and with dangerously uncertain control. That year, on the way to a modest 5–3 season, he struck out sixteen batters in a game, then the record (which he later broke with eighteen, unsurpassed until Steve Carlton, Tom Seaver, and Nolan Ryan struck out nineteen apiece). As he developed, his fastball was all he needed. In 1939, he won 24 games and notched 246 strikeouts; in 1940, 27 and 261; in 1941, 25 and 260. Then, as we used to chant, came the war.

After three years in service, he came back with a curve and a change to go with the fastball he could no longer throw with full velocity for nine innings. He went on to pitch for another twelve years, winning 26 games in 1946, 20 in 1947, and 22 in 1951. Two of his three no-hitters came after he started throwing more curves. In 1962 he was a shoo-in to the Hall of Fame.

Through the years since Candy Cummings, many small men have used the curve to put meat on the table. Consider what it has done to the longevity of present-day pitchers. In 1983, because of the nasty slider he perfected, Steve Carlton, at thirty-eight, became the highest paid pitcher in the history of the game. In 1982 he was the oldest man ever to lead the National League in strikeouts (286). As the 1983 season got started, Jim Kaat, at forty-four, began his twenty-fifth year in the majors and was working to add a new underhand fastball sinker to his other stuff. Joe Niekro, at thirty-nine, off a 1982 earned-run average of 2.47, was looking for his knuckler and other pitches to keep him in the game for as long a career as his brother Phil, who at forty-four was the knuckleball ace of the Atlanta Braves.

What the curveball means to baseball has been expressed at many a baseball banquet for years, in the form of the yarn about the young country boy trying to make a major league team in spring training. Daily, by postcard and letter, he reports to the folks back home on his good progress and high hopes, until one day they get this note: "Get out my work clothes, Mom. They've started to throw curve balls."

George Hildebrand, *left*, and Elmer Stricklett, in a 1961 reunion. In 1902 Hildebrand, a catcher and later for many years a major league umpire, showed Stricklett how to throw a spitter, and Stricklett took it to the majors with him. *The Sporting News*

Amos Rusie won
233 baseball
games in eight
seasons for the
New York
Giants. *The
Sporting News*

Denton True (Cy) Young, baseball's all-time winningest pitcher with 509 major league victories, including two no-hitters and one perfect game. *The Sporting News*

Nick Altrock, second from left in this photo taken in 1930 or 1931, said that if night baseball had existed in Johnson's time, Congress would have had to pass a law banning it. At left is Jack Chesbro; Bucky Harris is at right, next to Washington owner Clark Griffith. *International Photos*

Ty Cobb, fiercest of competitors, crowded the plate against Walter Johnson because he knew that the Big Train feared his fastball would maim an opponent. *The Sporting News*

CHAPTER TWO

The Ball in the Air

It can't be done. You cannot throw or bat a baseball that does not curve or change directions, if it is in the air long enough for its spin, or lack of spin, to take effect. If it spins, it will curve. Even a straight fastball pitch, or an over-the-top throw from the outfield straight to a base, is spinning upward to resist gravity. If spinless, the ball changes direction erratically.

The reality—the inevitability—of curve is unchallenged in other ball sports. Every golfer knows that a curving slice or sharp hook comes from the spin put on the ball, expertly or inadvertently, when the club head strikes it. Though it is against the holy rules of golf, habitual slicers could take a tip from baseball's unholy spitball and keep their drives in the fairway by coating the clubhead face with vaseline or casually wetting it with the morning dew. Every tennis player knows what the spin of a cut-shot does to the flight of the ball and its bounce.

In football, a properly kicked field goal attempt will rise with upward spin true to its aim; but the longer the try, the more any lateral spin will veer it or hook it away from the goal posts and three points on the board. But in baseball, the actuality of the curveball has been challenged ever since Candy Cummings first threw one. People (including degree-holding scientists, but not including the academically naive players, who merely throw it and try to hit it) have insisted that it is all, or mainly, an optical illusion.

In the early days of the game, physicists who saw the ball curve declared it impossible. Today they admit that a ball can be made to curve in a consistent arc; but, a sharp break? Impossible. Through the years scientists have monkeyed around with elaborate technology to demonstrate that a ball can or cannot be made to curve, and, if it does so, to measure how much and when. None of their reports is precisely reflective of curves thrown in actual game situations, and many are completely invalid. But since their measurements and reports have misled and confused a great many fans, they are an interesting part of the hokum—of which there is much—in the wonderful lore and history of baseball. The best of their analyses are flawed and the worst are absurd, because they do not reckon with the effects of the basic principles of aerodynamics upon a real baseball as thrown by a major league pitcher in a game situation or a valid approximation of one.

First, the ball itself. A baseball is not a ball is not a rose. Every throw in baseball is made with a ball that is not quite like any ball ever thrown before. Every thrown ball is as unique as a fingerprint. While fans and most professional players, including insensitive pitchers, assume that new balls are identical, the inherent characteristics of circumference, weight, and number and height of seams are actually (and officially) only approximately the same. Balls are different, too, because of what happens to them between throws. A ball that comes back to a pitcher with a grass stain or a scuffed surface will not behave exactly the same next time as it did on the previous pitch, even if the pitcher tries to throw it the same way. When the differences become significant—whether an accidental smoothness of stain or surface irregularity of scuff, or whether contrived, as with spit or a belt buckle—a sensitive and cunning pitcher can make the changed ball behave like a stranger from outer space.

There are almost always 108 full seams or 216 stitches on a ball, but no machine or human hand can sew them identically. Some seams and rows of seams are higher than others. Sensitive pitchers feel these differences and use them to increase, or diminish, the spin—or they reject the ball if they don't like its feel for a particular pitch. When a pitcher is "rubbing up" the ball, he is usually getting the feel of its seams. Harry (The Cat) Brecheen, who threw a variety of wicked curves, would often reject a new ball, a pitcher's prerogative. To test his fussiness, umpires would put the rejected ball in another pocket and later toss it back in the game; The Cat would disdain it again. A generation later, another St. Louis Cardinal pitcher, John Stuper, as a rookie was also fastidious. Whitey Herzog, never a pitcher, attributed John's rejections of new balls to the kid's getting himself into trouble with a batter. "When he starts asking for a different ball, you can see that he's nervous. I don't know if he doesn't want to throw it or what." But John rejected his boss's interpretation. "If I don't get a ball I like, I throw it back, that's all." It's fun to watch the many others who do, and see what kind of pitches they throw off seams that they like.

Some pitchers are also sensitive to the one-fourth of an inch allowance the major leagues permit in the minimum 9-inch circumference, and to the one-fourth-ounce variation in the required 5-ounce weight. A heavier, smaller ball will have more speed and less curve. Since 1976 both American League and National League balls are made to the same specifications by the Rawlings Company in Haiti, but for many years, going back to 1876, American League balls made by Reach had lower seams than those made by Spalding for the National League. This is why, traditionally, curveballers and junk-throwers found good homes in the National, while fastballers thrived in the American. Nowadays, with the same ball and with more interleague mobility of players, this interesting difference is leveling off.

Air, like water, is real stuff. Good pitchers, by seeing what their pitches are doing (and what batters are doing to them), adjust to the air pressure at the time of a game. Most games in our middle latitudes are played in barometric readings of from about 29.7 to 30.3 inches of mercury. In these normal ranges, the wind speed and direction will affect a pitch of 60 feet, and infield throws across the diamond, much more than will air pressure (the weight and thickness of air). But abnormally high pressure adds curve to spinning balls and takes a foot or two off fastballs, while very low pressure causes curves to hang and fastballs to get there quicker. A difference of even a few hundredths of an inch of pressure can make the difference between a hit and an out in balls hit to the outfield, and a safe-or-out difference to throws coming back. Updrafts, downdrafts, and sudden turbulence—which are different in each ballpark—compound variations of pressure.

A dramatic effect of sudden change in air pressure on the outcome of a game could be seen in the eighth and ninth innings of a game between the Cardinals, at home, and the San Francisco Giants on Sunday afternoon, May 1, 1983. There were severe thunderstorms and destructive tornadoes reported for 200 miles to the south and west of St. Louis. The radio account of the game was frequently interrupted by weather bureau warnings of approaching storms. After seven innings, with the Cards ahead 9–4, I got more interested in the weather than the game. I checked my barometer (a lingering habit from Air Force training as a weather observer), noting a reading of 29.72 inches, and went out into my yard, a few miles west of Busch Stadium, to watch the turbulence in the sky—a chaotic mixture of scudding low clouds, swirling middle clouds, and advancing anvil heads, interspersed with patches of blue and glimpses of sunshine. Watching the weather and listening to the radio on the porch, I heard Jack Buck and Mike Shannon's account of how the Giants scored twice in their half of the eighth, making the score 9–6, with two runners on base and one out. But Whitey Herzog of the Cardinals called for Bruce Sutter, and he got the next outs with his sharp-sinking forkball. The Cards got one run back in the bottom of the eighth. As Bruce went back to the mound with a four-run lead, I hoped we were as safe from the storm as the Cards were from defeat.

The thunder from the streaks of lightning in the west was seven seconds away, then five, then three. I checked the barometer. In fifteen minutes it had dropped more than four hundredths of an inch, to 29.32. And whack, whack, whack—the Giant bats seemed to make as much noise as the thunder. In the suddenly lighter air, the downspin on Bruce's sinker was not taking. His sinking fastball was just a plain fastball, and hits were streaking off the bats like the lightning. Bruce gave up five hits and three runs, and had the tying run on third and the losing run on first before Johnny LeMaster of the Giants grounded to third for the final out. None of the 42,000 fans in the stands, nor the reporters, nor the coaches or players, was aware of the invisible change in air pressure that turned the Cardinal breeze into a sudden Giant storm. But it was the air pressure that did it.

Probably the most famous demonstration of the effect of air on a baseball took place on August 21, 1908, when Gabby Street, catcher for the Senators, caught a ball, on his thirteenth try, tossed from the top of the Washington Monument. Fans who acclaimed his catch believed that the speed of the descending ball made it so difficult, but it wasn't that at all. In a vacuum, the ball would have had a velocity of 179 feet per second when it hit Gabby's mitt, but it actually came to him at only 140 feet per second, a little slower than the Walter Johnson fastballs he was catching routinely.

What caused his twelve misses was that the toss quickly lost its spin and came down like a crazy knuckler—the Bernoulli Effect on a spinless object in laminar flow. Daniele Bernoulli, a Swiss physicist, reported in 1728 the surprising phenomenon that the pressure within a fluid flow is less than the pressure around it. The air pressure within the funnel of a tornado, to take a horrendous example, is much less than that within the strong winds around it. This is why a house with, say, internal pressure of 30 inches, explodes when the immeasurably low pressure within the funnel sweeps down and across it. The surrounding strong winds may scatter the debris far and freakishly, but the destruction is caused by the low pressure within the vortex.

To amaze the children and yourself with a parlor trick, stick a common pin as a stabilizer through a calling card and put the pin in the hole of a spool of thread; now, holding the card in place, blow into the other end of the spool and take away your supporting finger. The harder you try to blow it away, the more firmly the card will stick to the end of the spool, because the air pressure in the parlor is greater on the outside of the card than that of the air you are blowing against it; stop blowing and the card falls away. The Bernoulli Effect applies to laminar, or streamlined, flow on a spinless object such as an airplane wing or the sail on a boat; the airplane and boat move in the direction of lesser pressure within the flow of air. This is why heavy airplanes fly and boats tack against the wind. It is also why knucklers take sudden zips as the seams on the ball sway one way or the other.

More than a century after Bernoulli, Heinrich G. Wagner, a German physicist, trying to figure out why cannon shots were curving off target, arrived at the Wagner Effect on spinning objects in a flow of air or water. The spin creates turbulent flow that increases the differences of pressure within the flow. On a boat, the propeller creates lesser pressure in front, and the boat moves forward. A spinning ball moves up, down, or sideways, depending upon where (on which side) the spin is creating less pressure.

In the most plausible and realistic study of the curveball I have been able to find and which I will review later on, the late Lyman J. Briggs, a distinguished scientist, explains the inevitability of curve this way:

Let us imagine that the spinning ball with its rough seams creates around itself a kind of whirlpool of air that stays with the ball when it is thrown into still air, but the picture is easier to follow if we imagine that the ball is not moving forward but that the wind is flowing past it. The relative motions are the same. On one side of the ball, the motions of the wind and the whirlpool are in the same directions, and the whirlpool is speeded up. On the opposite side of the ball, the whirlpool is moving against the wind and is slowed down. . . . On the side of the spinning ball where the velocity of the whirlpool has been increased, the air pressure has been reduced; and on the opposite side, it has been increased. This difference in pressure tends to push the ball sidewise or make it curve.

The first formal verification of a pitched curve was made on August 16, 1870, at the long-gone Capitoline Ballpark in Brooklyn. Henry (Father) Chadwick, a man more important in the development of today's type of game than anyone else who never played it, heard about a young fellow named Fred Goldsmith who could make a ball curve in its 45-foot flight from the pitcher's box to the plate. Chadwick was also aware that the physicists were saying it could not be done. He challenged Goldsmith, one of the claimants to being first to throw a curve, to prove it.

Accepting the challenge, Goldsmith was confronted with two stakes set 20 feet apart in a line from the center of the box to the center of the plate. As Chadwick marveled and the crowd cheered, Goldsmith threw half a dozen pitches to the right of the first stake and to the left of the second. Everybody there—like the Missourian who was asked if he believed in baptism—could say, "Hell, yes. I've seen it done."

But many physicists, aloof from baseball actuality, discounted Chadwick's report with the theory of optical illusion, and their skepticism persists to this day. Because they were reported in respected magazines of national circulation, the three best-known studies of the curveball are those printed by *Life*, *Look*, and *Science 82*. Their conclusion that it is all, or mainly, an optical illusion was based on photographs and measurements of balls pitched in situations that were no more like actual game situations than a handsaw is like a hawk, to use an old Missouri metaphor.

For its report in its issue of September 15, 1941, *Life* got Gjon Mili, an expert high-speed photographer, to photograph pitches thrown indoors in the dark at a backstop in front of a plate painted on the floor. The pitchers were two renowned curveballers, Cy Blanton of the Phillies, a righthander, and lefty King Carl Hubbell himself, then in his fourteenth year with the Giants as the game's premier screwball pitcher. Okay so far? No! First of all, they were not pitching to the target of a batter standing up or back in his box, a catcher calling for specific placement, and a crouching umpire, all of whom are essential to give the pitcher the perspective to throw an effective pitch; second, neither the pictures nor the verbal report indicate that they were throwing from a mound, the height of which may be among the most important inches in baseball.

Mili synchronized three cameras—one from somewhere above the plate, one from somewhere behind whatever backstop was used, and one from somewhere on the side. The pitches, thrown indoors, were photographed simultaneously at one-thirtieth of a second intervals between flashes. Beyond an arching fall, attributed entirely to gravity, the blobs of balls, as printed, came in on an uncurving line. King Carl's screwball was photographed coming in straight. So were Cy's out-breaking curve and his in-breaking screwball.

"Possibly there is an infinitely small side movement of the ball," said *Life*, "but these pictures fail to show it." The reason there is no curve, *Life* went on, and that "this standby of baseball is after all only an optical illusion," is that no pitcher "has a strong enough finger and wrist motion to put the necessary spin on the ball which would materially affect its sidewise motion."

Gratuitously, since his pitches were not involved, *Life* went on to conclude that "the hop on Bobby Feller's fastball is another example of a batter's optical illusion." (Feller had just used this "optical illusion" to strike out a league-leading 260 batters on the way to 25 wins.) *Life* did not measure or report on the velocity of the pitches thrown by Blanton and Hubbell, nor did it try to count rotation, which, with 12 to 20 presumably sharp pictures of each pitch, it might have been able to do. *Life*'s conclusion of an optical illusion confirmed in the minds of scoffers the theory that the curveball was the myth of dumb athletes; it also confused and dismayed nonplaying fans. Players from sandlots to the major leagues hooted their derision: "What did you hit?" "A hanging optical illusion," the home run hitter would tell his mates. "Well, that's *Life* for you."

Twelve years later *Look* took a swipe at it. Noting that high-speed photography and wind tunnel technology had been much improved in the meantime, *Look* engaged the same Mili to take pictures of lefty Ken Raffensberger's tantalizing curves. This time Mili set up three open-shutter cameras, one 50 feet above a painted plate (a position from which no pitcher, batter, umpire, or fan has ever seen a major league pitch), one at the side to measure velocity, and a third on the other side to photograph rotation. They painted half the ball black, the better to see and count its spins. Indoors in the dark, Kenny threw this grossly illegal "shine" ball down a beam of light (from a mound?) while the cameras photographed its flight. A good picture shows Kenny's four-seam grip with the "shine" side to the left, which would greatly reduce air pressure on the surface where the ball's spin (the Wagner Effect) would enhance it, thus diminishing curve.

The side pictures of the ball in flight show it rising from release and falling in a gentle arc toward the plate. The view from above shows a gentler lateral arc going out (away from a righthanded batter), about six inches at 30 feet and then back to the center of the plate, a curve that a Little Leaguer could clobber. From the photos and calculations, *Look* came to these conclusions: "Mili's film shows some surprising new scientific facts: a curve ball . . . spins at 1400 revolutions per minute, a far greater rate than anyone thought possible . . . but its speed was surprisingly slow . . . a curve moves at only 43 MPH. . . . Yes, a curve ball does curve, but in a gentle arc. No, a curve ball does not 'break.' "

Here is what Stan Musial had to say about Kenny's curves: "Raffy had nothing but slow stuff and a forkball, but with changing speeds and control, he made those pitches seem so fat when they weren't . . . looked as big as a grapefruit but fell off the table, low. The challenge of going for the long ball off soft stuff hurt me against Raffy."

The 43-MPH curve that *Look* clocked was not "surprisingly slow," but about the average speed of most major league slow curves. And the 1400 RPM that *Look* counted was a good deal less than the 1700 RPM that good curveballers are believed to achieve routinely, although no one has yet come up with a way to measure rotation (or curve or break, for that matter) in a game situation.

Look turned Mili's pictures and its own calculations over to Joseph Bickwell, a professor of aeronautical engineering at M.I.T. He put a ball on a rotator set at 1400 RPM in a 43-MPH blow of air in a wind tunnel, and measured the curve thrust of its spin. *Look* said that his findings, which were based on illegal junk thrown in the dark by a slow pitch artist, scientifically supported its generalizations about the behavior of all curves, a pronouncement which got the same derisive hoot from baseball people that *Life's* report had provoked.

Thirty years later, the magazine *Science 82* took its shot at the curve. Robert G. Watts, of the Department of Engineering at Tulane University, was engaged (on the basis of an elaborate but inconsequential wind tunnel study of the knuckleball he had made in 1974–75), along with Jim Watson, identified as a computer-graphics specialist from the Biomedical Science Division of General Motors, and Charles Miller, an expert in high-speed photography and strobe lighting from M.I.T. To do the throwing for the experiment, they got two good major leaguers from the Baltimore Orioles—Ray Miller, pitching coach, a righthander, and Scott McGregor, a lefty, both known for their breaking stuff and neither for throwing smoke.

Like *Life* and *Look*, they set up a darkened indoor pitching tunnel. To delineate the tunnel and to serve as coordinates, they hung five pairs of ping pong balls on both sides, each pair 15 feet apart, from the pitching slab to the painted plate. (Again, no realistic target.) From the photos, 120 of them a second, Watson was able to make computer graphs of the pitches accurate "within a tenth of an inch." Both pitchers were instructed to throw only over-the-top sinkers (although high-speed color photography of Ray's delivery motion shows partial lateral spin). No effort was made to photograph or plot any curve direction except down, nor to measure velocity or to count RPM.

The pictures, graphs, and conclusions were heralded on the cover of the November, 1982, issue as "Secrets of the Curve—What Baseball Doesn't Know." The report, written by a staffer named William P. Allman, was headed "Pitching Rainbows—the untold physics of the curve ball." His report is unworthy of a magazine, whether called *Science* or by any other name. He does not tell us whether the graphs—accurate, remember, to "within a tenth of an inch"—are based on the best pitch thrown by either Miller or Scott, or on a composite of all of them, and, if so, how many. He mentions flight time of .4 seconds and "about half a second"—velocities at which no sinker curve has ever been or could be thrown. Even more disconcerting is the fact that neither Allman nor Professor Watts, in his interpretation of the experiment, is aware of, or believes, what the definitive computer graph, as printed, actually shows.

Allman writes that the spin on the sinker caused a drop in its flight of about a foot more than can be attributed to gravity. "A pitch that takes only .4 seconds to reach the catcher," he continues, ignoring that there was no catcher, and contemplating a pitch of more than 100 MPH, "drops only six inches in the first half of flight, but it drops more than two feet in the second half. Still, the motion is gradual, and there is no sharp break. . . . What appears to be a movement greater in the second half than in the first . . . occurs because the batter is standing near the circle formed by the curving ball." He likens it to a viewer watching a train approach on a circular track: "The train at first appears to be travelling in a straight line, and then appears to be moving sideways as it passes. . . . This illusion is what causes the apparent break in a curveball."

Watts, also ignoring what the computer graph shows, tries to reconcile his no-break theory with what batters know that they see. The findings, he says, show that both physicists and batters can now say, "I told you so." Yes, "it's falling off the table," but "the curving force is taking an absolute circular path. . . . There is no way the force can suddenly take effect ten feet from the plate."

This is what the computer graph, as printed, actually shows: At about 20 feet, the ball is about five inches higher than when released. At 30 feet it is at the same height, not six inches lower. In the next 15 feet, it drops about ten inches and is now only 15 feet from the plate. In the last 15 feet it drops another foot, and in the last five feet sinks as much as it did in the previous ten. While the ball, as shown by the graph, did not "break" in the sense that it changed direction at an angle, it broke sharply in terms of baseball meaning. Its final dip would be like that of a roller coaster taking a sudden 30-degree downward swerve without leaving its track. Such is the "secret of the curve," which baseball already knew.

In his earlier study, with Eric Sawyer at Tulane University, Watts set up a rotatable stationary ball, affixed with pressure-measuring devices, in a wind tunnel "to determine precisely the forces that cause the erratic motion of a knuckleball." The report, complete with mathematical formulas and graphs, was published in the November, 1975, issue of *American Journal of Physics*. It confirmed what effective knuckleballers and their victims already knew—that a nearly spinless ball, one that rotates less than once, breaks more, and more erratically, than one that rotates two or three times or that does not rotate at all. In the tunnel, they could blow air against a completely spinless ball. But every completely spinless ball thrown in an actual baseball game inevitably rotates somewhat in response to the air flow on its seams. Such a nearly spinless ball, the two scientists reported, "will take a sudden change in curvature . . . the deflecting force is erratic." But, having described what baseball people call, and swing at as, a break, unswervingly true to their cult of physics they state: "No break occurs."

More than twenty years earlier, in a similar wind tunnel demonstration at the University of Iowa, C. H. McCloy, of the physical education department, and Elmer Lundquist, professor of engineering, showed that a knuckler does indeed take a sudden, sharp downward break as it nears the plate. What happens aerodynamically, they say, is this: "When the ball leaves the pitcher's hand, it runs head on into a 'wall' of air. This air pushes at the front of the ball and pulls at the back. The air also tends to 'pile up' on the seams and rough surfaces. The forces holding the ball back build up so fast that the ball slows down suddenly and drops unusually fast . . . usually a short distance in front of the plate and causes the batter to swing 'where it was, not where it is.' "

Had ballplayers heard about this obscure report, an amen would have resounded throughout the land.

The scorn that ballplayers entertained for the credibility of the 1953 *Look* report came, somehow, to the attention of Igor Sikorsky, then absorbed in developing the helicopter for United Aircraft. He called for Ralph Lightfoot, a wind tunnel specialist: "Look, Mr. Lightfoot, here we have a solid object, moving rapidly in space and rotating on a vertical axis. You see? The question is, can it elude the man with the stick?"

In their wind tunnel, with sensitive measuring devices affixed to a ball rotating at different speeds in various wind velocities, they found, aerodynamically, that an artificially contrived curveball of 80 MPH curves as much as 19 inches when thrown with the equivalent of the four-seam grip used by many curveballers. Though its intelligibility can be apparent to only mathematically trained ballplayers, Sikorsky's formula for determining the effects of variables, including air pressure, on the amount of curve in feet is as follows:

$$d = \frac{{}^cL \; P \; V^2 \; t^2 \; g \; C^2}{7230 \; W} \; feet$$

Where; d equals displacement from a straight line; ${}^cL$ equals circulation of air generated by friction when ball is spinning; P equals the density of the air (normal at .002378); V equals the speed of the ball; t equals the time for delivery; g equals the acceleration of gravity (32.2 feet per second^2); C equals the circumference of the ball (9 inches); and W equals the ball's weight (.3125 pounds); while the number 7230 relates other values of pounds, inches, feet, seconds, etc., to arrive at an answer in feet.

It was the aforementioned Dr. Briggs—a lifelong fan, then (in 1958) eighty-four years old and director emeritus of the National Bureau of Standards and director of research for the National Geographic Society—who made a great try at measuring the effects of speed and spin on curves in a gamelike situation.

After carrying out wind tunnel measurements similar to Sikorsky's, he went to the mound and plate at old Griffith Stadium. With the help of Cookie Lavagetto, then a coach for the Washington Senators, he studied the pitches thrown to catcher Ed Fitzgerald by Pedro Ramos and Camilo Pasqual, both righthanded pitchers.

To measure spin, he fastened a light tape to the ball, stretched it from slab to plate, and counted the twists in the tape as rotations. However light the tape and uninhibitive to delivery, it would have had some unrealistic effect, but no better count of the spin of an actual pitch has been made. Putting his measurements at Griffith Stadium and in the wind tunnel together, he concluded that "the speed of the pitch has little effect on the amount it curves; the important thing is the amount of spin." He calculated, for example, that increasing the rotation from 1200 RPM to 1800 RPM on 68-MPH pitches increases curve from about 12 inches to 18 inches; increasing the speed up to 100 MPH at these rotations has no effect on the amount of curve. Pitches of 85 MPH and 100 MPH, both spinning at 1200 RPM, curve 11.5 inches each. Thus, pitchers like Walter Johnson, Bob Feller, Nolan Ryan, etc., who can put good spin on their fastballs, can make them "move"—up, down, or sideways. So, from their fingers on the seams, the fastballs of the great masters become a kind of curveball, too.

The most determined exponent of the Optical Illusion explanation was Ernest Lowry, a Canadian. He maintained in a barrage of press releases that the "curve pitch" was a connivance on the part of baseball profiteers "to trick the press into hoodwinking the public on this ballyhoo feature of the national game." He was "nauseated" by the "trash" in books for young ballplayers "which have flooded the United States, Canada, and other countries" containing "curve pitch instructions." He was contemptuous of "the despicable brand of sportsmanship reflected in taking penny-bank savings from fine young boys for such 'instructions' in pitching."

In July of 1952, he suggested legal proceedings: "The American and Canadian governments have just completed ratification of an agreement to the Extradition Treaty under which fraud is an extraditable offense in both countries. While the new agreement is primarily aimed at protecting Americans against being sold worthless Canadian stocks, it could also mean that anyone in the United States selling fraudulent books on pitching may be arrested and extradited to stand trial in Canadian courts."

It would have been a dandy trial, but unfortunately no prosecutor proceeded on this premise. But a sportswriter discussed Lowry's insistence that the curve was a hoax with Eddie Sawyer, former manager of the Philadelphia Phillies.

"I am not positive whether a ball curves or not," said Eddie, "but if this pitch does not curve, it would be well to notify a lot of baseball players who were forced to quit the game they love because of this pitch and may now be reached at numerous gas stations, river docks, and mental institutions."

Christy Mathewson, who threw three World Series shutouts against the Philadelphia Athletics in 1905 for John McGraw's New York Giants, called his screwball the "fadeaway." *The Sporting News*

John J. McGraw, the "Little Napoleon," who threatened to put a surgeon to work on the throwing hands of New York Giant pitchers. *The Sporting News*

Mordecai (Three-Finger) Brown, Matty's nemesis, could do strange and wonderful things with a curveball. *The Sporting News*

Walter Johnson, the "Big Train" of the Washington Senators. He could throw so fast that he didn't even need a curveball. *The Sporting News*

CHAPTER THREE

And in the Beginning . . .

Baseball became the fascinating game we call our national pastime because of the existence of curveballs and crooked pitches. Without these deceptions, there would be no great hitters. Without the curve, the tough decisions of the game would be happy-go-lucky happenstance. Without the possibility of a curve, baseball would have remained a game played for fun and exercise by amateurs.

The stories of the origins, development, and uses of the various curveballs, legal and illegal, constitute inseparable fibers in the gaudy fabric of the game's lore, legend, and history. And, as Paul Mac Farlane puts it, "the essence of baseball is its historicity." You can look it up.

You could look it up and learn, for example—as did John Duxbury of the *St. Louis Post-Dispatch* sports staff—that Joaquin Andujar broke a Cardinal record as a batter in 1982–83 by striking out forty-four times without drawing a walk, twelve more times than Lee Meadows did in 1916, but that he did not equal the major league record set in 1970 by Gaylord Perry, who struck out forty-seven times before getting a base on balls.

There are legions of fans who devote themselves, both professionally and as hobbyists, to painstaking original research into the records of the game and its players. Some delve into old tomes in solitary curiosity, while others dig in organized fellowship with their research peers. One distinguished fellowship of this bent is the Society for American Baseball Research, which publishes a scholarly journal, *The National Pastime.* Its members are zealously concerned with the accuracy of the records that are such a big and detailed part of baseball history. They seek and tear into inaccuracies like terriers grabbing rats.

I accept as gospel the *Sporting News* figures showing, for example, that Cy Young won 511 major league games and that Walter Johnson won 416. But a dedicated researcher like Frank J. Williams does not. Reporting in *The National Pastime,* "derived from year-by-year and game-by-game studies of the official scoring sheets housed in the Baseball Hall of Fame Library," he counts 510 for Young and 417 for Johnson.

There is sure to be a research rhubarb when and if Pete Rose closes in on Ty Cobb's record for most hits in the major leagues. How many hits should Ty really be credited with? 4189? 4190? 4191? The fur is going to fly.

My fun as a fan comes not from verifying the secondhand numbers I accept, but in conjuring from them the mind and heart, the skill and stamina of the players who fielded, ran, batted, and pitched them, out in open play to the cheers and jeers of the multitude, into the silent cemeteries of often contradictory record books.

With all its detailed records and authentic history, much of the lore and legend of baseball is, as Old Henry Ford said of all history, the bunk. Fact and myth have become intertwined—as they have in all great endeavors of war and peace—to create lore and legends of heroics never performed, of events that never happened, and of undeserved attributions, much of which will live as truth forever in the hearts and minds of fans, and some of which are imbedded in the official history of the game. And, in the way of the world, some of the great heroics and innovations in the game as it began and was developed are undusted for their shining truth, their heroes unsung when legends are told.

So it is with the curveball, the most significant innovation, along with the 90-foot diamond, in the history of the game. Candy Cummings is enshrined in the Hall of Fame as its innovator. But was he? Or is that all bunk, too—like the myth that Babe Ruth pointed to the place over the wall where he was going to hit Charley Root's next pitch in the fifth inning of the third game of the World Series of 1932? Or that Abner Doubleday invented baseball by laying out a 90-foot diamond at Cooperstown? A good case can be made for Candy, but the fantasies of Babe calling his shot and Cooperstown as the birthplace of baseball are the kind of bunk that has replaced the more interesting truth in the history and lore of the game. Before reviewing the contributions of some of the innovators and their documented recollections, it is fun to see how so much myth has become accepted as authentic lore.

That day in 1932 at Wrigley Field, the Cub bench and the fans in the temporary bleacher stands in shortened rightfield were razzing the Babe for a crack he had made, coming into town with two victories under the Yankee belts, that the Cubs were a bunch of cheapskates for voting ex-Yankee shortstop Mark Koenig, traded to the Cubs late in the season, only a half-share of their World Series winnings. The fans were tossing sour lemons to the Babe's feet. Unruffled by the fans, the Babe tossed them back and belted a home run. But when it appeared to the Cubs that their needling was getting under the Babe's tough skin, they kept jabbing away.

They jeered and hooted when Root fired a strike past Ruth in the fifth. When Root fired strike two, the crescendo of taunts was orchestrated by another rolling lemon. Ruth turned to the Cub bench and swept a pointed finger at it, hollering against the jeers that it only takes one to hit it.

It is history that he homered on the next pitch, and the mythmakers in the press box and thousands of fans in the stands, unaware of the final direction of the Babe's defiant gesture, believed and reported that he pointed to the spot in centerfield where he was going to belt the ball. It was too good a story to disbelieve, and the myth became part of the mightiest hero's legend.

It never was established whether the ball went into the temporary stands in rightfield, over them, or to the left of them, but it did not even occur to any of the principals, including Root and catcher Gabby Hartnett, that the Babe was calling his shot.

Root, whose 201 victories for the Cubs (1926–41) were earned in part by his high, tight pitches to aggressive batters, scoffed at the myth; had the Babe been calling his shot, he would have had to take that swing with his backside in the dirt. It is out of respect for Ruth's professionalism that most baseball people concur with Root and Hartnett; they cannot believe that he would be guilty of such bush league showboating.

Asked about it years later, Bob Gibson put it this way: "If I thought anybody did a bush thing like that on me, I would stick the ball in one of his ears and out the other."

In the clamor that followed the Babe's homer, the real heroics of that moment in baseball were all but lost. As Lou Gehrig stepped from the on-deck circle to be the first to congratulate him, Ruth said under the thunder of the crowd: "Why don't you do the same thing?" Lou replied, "I will." He did, and it was quiet Lou, in a private exchange, who called his shot that day.

A myth you will find recorded as fact in the encyclopedias is that Abner Doubleday "invented" baseball in 1839 by laying out the 90-foot geometry of the diamond in the place where the Hall of Fame now stands in Cooperstown, New York. How this bit of bunk was muscled by Albert Goodwill Spalding against documented fact into revered truth is as interesting as the real story. He was able to do it mainly because Americans wanted to believe that their beloved game owed nothing at all to the Old World, especially England. But all the later developments and refinements, including the deception of the curve, that have made it our national pastime are rooted in its evolutionary origins, many of which persist in alleys and sandlots everywhere in this favored land.

In perhaps the best account of the game's origins, Robert W. Henderson (*Ball, Bat, and Bishop*, Rockport Press, 1947) traces the evolution of baseball from ancient Egyptian ball and stick games to English cricket and to the "rounders" variations that British colonists brought to New England and the New York area. In rounders, the first step to the curveball came as the ball was thrown in the air to the batter, not bowled as in cricket. So it was a pitching, batting, running, and fielding game in which several defenders tried (and still do in kids' sandlot games) to end the life of one old cat at the plate. (There is a farfetched belief that "one old cat" is derived from a two-stick game called "one hole cat.") Two, three, and four old cats and two and three bases were added. The fun of the game increased as margins between "safe" and "out" were refined. A three-base game played by grown men had emerged as "town ball," when, in 1845, Alexander Cartwright, a New York surveyor, laid out a diamond 30 yards and 15 inches on a side, which was quickly standardized at an even 90 feet. (How many thousands of batters who beat out throws to first at 90 feet would have been thrown out if they had had to go the extra fifteen inches of Cartwright's original specifications?) The 4-foot square pitcher's box was 45 feet from home plate. Under the rules Cartwright drafted, the pitcher stood in the box facing the batter. He could step forward in the box to pitch but could not release the ball above his waist or break his wrist. Thus at most only a rainbow drop curve was legally possible.

The first formal baseball game was played on June 19, 1846, on the Elysian Field in Hoboken, New Jersey, when Cartwright's Knickerbockers took on the New York Baseball Club. As his pitcher went to the box, Cartwright told him to "let them hit it, you've got your fielders behind you." The Knickerbockers were clobbered 23 to 1.

But Spalding prevailed against history and obtained official certification that baseball was the purely American invention of Doubleday at Cooperstown in 1839. Spalding declared that baseball "must be free from the trammels of English traditions, customs, and conventionalities. . . . Baseball is the exponent of American Courage, Confidence, Combatitiveness; American Dash, Discipline, Determination; American Energy, Eagerness, Enthusiasm."

As a pitcher (who never threw a curve), club owner, and manufacturer, Spalding had clout in the baseball world. He had pitched all 31 games that Boston of the National Association played in 1871, when he became the first 20-game winner and pitched the first one-hitter. He was owner of the Chicago National League club from 1882 to 1891. The A. G. Spalding & Bros. company he founded in 1876 was for many years the dominant equipment supplier. Since there is no indication of Irishness in his names, his anti-English oratory may have been, by jingo, pure American patriotism. It was also very good for business.

In 1905, he called for the formation of a special commission, made up of politicians not associated with baseball, to establish the origin of the game "in some comprehensive and authoritative way for all time." In choosing Doubleday as its originator, he had red-blooded America on his side. A West Pointer, Doubleday fought in the glamorous (back home) Mexican War and heard the first shots of the Civil War at Fort Sumter. His heroism at Gettysburg is memorialized by his statue on the battlefield. He came out of the war a major general. Since he had been resting in Arlington Cemetery since 1893, he was unable to testify about any part he may have had in inventing baseball. It was one Abner Graves, then in his nineties and harking back two-thirds of a century, who testified that yes, he had seen it done. A. G. Mills, an Army buddy of Doubleday and a member of the commission, added his aye, and Spalding's ayes had it—Doubleday, Cooperstown, 1839.

Of Spalding's triumph, Father Chadwick shook his aged head and said the only game played then in Cooperstown was four old cat. "In the language of Dead Eye Dick," he said of Spalding, "he means well, but he don't know." Of the commission's decision, Branch Rickey later said: "The only thing Doubleday invented was the Civil War."

Fred Lieb, a retired member of *The Sporting News* staff, recalled in a letter to Paul Mac Farlane being assigned in 1938–39 by Taylor Spink, then publisher, to go to Cooperstown to get the full story of the origin of the game in connection with the forthcoming celebration of its centennial there. Browsing around town, he could find no one—at the Chamber of Commerce, the weekly newspaper, or among venerable citizens—"who had the haziest notion why Cooperstown was being honored as the birthplace of baseball except 'they say baseball was first played here.' " Looking into historical records about Doubleday, he learned that the hero-to-be was out of town being a plebe at West Point at the time he was "inventing" the game. So he called up his boss and said, "Taylor, I've got a hell of a story here. This Cooperstown-Doubleday origin is a gigantic hoax, if not a fraud. I'll write that if Doubleday were still alive, he would be the most surprised man in town to learn that he invented baseball here."

But Mr. Spink cut in: "Oh, no, Fred. We just can't do that. They named me on the committee to celebrate baseball's first hundred years. Write the story as if you had no suspicions, and don't knock Doubleday."

So, Fred says, he made up a story putting Doubleday "at the scene of the crime. I had him visiting relatives and drawing a baseball field on the Cooperstown turf." Thus myth becomes history.

Speaking of myth, joyless Mudville, where mighty Casey struck out, is as historic in my heart as Cooperstown. And there *was* a Mudville—a station stop not far from San Francisco where Ernest L. Thayer wrote the Casey epic. It was published first, obscurely, on Sunday morning, June 3, 1888, in the *San Francisco Daily Examiner.*

Was "Casey at the Bat" based on an actual game and a real-life batter nicknamed Casey? Who knows, really? But there is factual substance to the legend that it was Candy Cummings who first made a baseball curve.

Arthur William Cummings was born in Ware, Massachusetts, on October 17, 1848, two years and four months after the first game of record was played on Elysian Field. He was fourteen when "the idea and inspiration" of throwing a curveball came to him. Idly, he picked up a clam shell and threw it. Watching its curving flight, "I thought what a wonderful thing it would be if I could make a baseball curve like that." His playmates teased him as he fooled around with ways to put curving spin on his nickel rocket ball. "I will find a way and strike you all out," he responded.

Information on his early experiments and his later achievements as a pro is derived from an interview he gave *The Sporting News* at seventy-four, printed December 29, 1921, two years before his death, and from a more detailed story Harold C. Burr wrote for the November 19, 1942, issue that was based in part on research by Guy Smith of Danville, Illinois, "a painstaking, thorough, and respected digger into the dusty archives of the game."

For four years, as he got his full growth to 5' 9" and 120 pounds, Arthur worked away at the curve, and first saw the ball take a quick swerve in 1864. Though he knew it was the deception a little guy would need, he kept it secret. "I was jealous of it and did not want anyone to crib it." He got his best curves by holding the ball toward the end of his fingers "in a death grip" and, throwing underhand, releasing it with a quick wrist-turn. Though the turn of the wrist was against the rules of Organized Ball, he got by with it in 1866, first with the Fulton Hercules and then with the Excelsior Juniors of Brooklyn.

While pitching 21 games in 1866 and 1867 (no won-loss record available) for the Juniors, Arthur (not yet known as Candy) labored at developing a dependable curve. Once he lost the knack for a month; then he got it back "as suddenly as it went, this time to stay." Because of his "death grip," he wore a kid glove on his pitching hand to keep his fingertips from blistering; otherwise his hand would become "a ragged wreck after a few innings."

He told no one, not even his catcher, what he was trying to make the ball do. The catcher played back to catch the ball off the ground and was in no danger of getting crossed up by a curve. Arthur was irked by the batter's advantage of being able to signal for a "fair" pitch, high or low, but, working corners, made good use of the nine "balls" it took for the batter to walk. Toward the end of the 1867 season, he made public claim of his mastery of the curve and said he would prove it in a game against Harvard, whose students and teachers of physics jeered at his boast when he went to the box. But, he recalled, "I curveballed them to death."

During the next four years he pitched 59 games (still no won-loss record) for the Star Club of Brooklyn. Up with the New York Mutuals of the National Association in 1872, he pitched 53 games, racking up a 34–19 record. No respecter of contracts, he took best offers around the National Association, pitching for Baltimore in 1873 (43 games, 29–14), Philadelphia in 1874 (54, 28–26), and Hartford in 1875 (52, 34–11, with an earned-run average, which Father Chadwick's scoring system had made computable, of 1.73).

"Art was artful," Burr wrote. "On wet days he would squeeze the pulpy horsehide, and the ball, in addition to its curve, would come up to the batter lop-sided. He would feign indifference and weariness to catch the opposition off-guard. Cummings didn't send up a roundhouse curve, but, rather, a sharp-breaking hook that barely eluded the lashing bats of those grandpas of the game. He became a mysterious terror. He had the fans on a hot seat, and many arguments and fist fights were started in the bleachers."

Art's best year was 1876, when the Hartford Dark Blues went into the new National League. He pitched 24 games, won 16, 5 with shutouts, losing 8, with an ERA of 1.66. His National League debut, a shutout against St. Louis, was one of the all-time beauties. Of the 27 outs, 24 were pop-ups, 21 to the catcher and 3 to Art.

In 1876, with one of their starters out of action, Bob Ferguson, Hartford manager, called upon him to pitch a doubleheader against the Cincinnati Redlegs. He beat Dale Williams 14–4 in the first and Dory Dean 8–4 in the second. The Hartford Historical Society declared him to be the first to win a doubleheader, but Ferguson said it all: "God never gave him any size, but he's the candy."

When the last pitching restrictions were removed in 1887, such stronger-armed pitchers as Jim "Deacon" White, Tom Bond, Jack Manning, and Frank Larkin, now able to throw an overhand sinker, outshone Candy as a pitching star. Batters jumped on his relatively simple stuff. In his last National League year, for the Redlegs, he was 5–14 with no shutouts. He stayed on in baseball to pitch in the minors and to become president of the International Association, the first formal minor league.

Candy was not the only "iron man" of his era. Others who were practically one-man staffs were Tim Keefe, Smiling Mickey Welsh, Jim Galvin, Charley "Old Hoss" Radbourn, and John Montgomery Ward.

The Iron Men of yore are no more. Hub Kittle says it's because of the new breed of mound specialists: "Today you've got special guys for righties, for lefties, for power hitters, for line-drive hitters. You've got long relievers and short relievers. Pitchers used to pace themselves. They wouldn't strike anybody out until they tried to. They'd have better stuff in the ninth than in the first. The proudest thing in baseball is walkin' to the dugout after the last out, knowin' that, 'Baby, I did it.' Something you did and didn't have help from nobody. You took it by the horns and you did it! That's pride, my friend."

The end of the Iron Man era could be marked by the longest major league game ever played—the 1 to 1 tie, called by darkness, between the Dodgers and the Braves on May 1, 1920. Both Leon Cadore and Joe Oeschger pitched all of the 26 innings for their teams.

It was not the pitching—Iron Man or relief—but the perfection of the fielding that impressed Candy Cummings the most in the last major league game he saw, in 1921 at Fenway Park (Red Sox vs. Browns), three years before his death. "It's too perfect," he said of the errorless play. "Errors are a part of the excitement. It wasn't like this when I was pitching."

There were other claimants, with interesting support, for being the first curveballer. When Father Chadwick called upon Fred Goldsmith to bend his curve around the stakes in Brooklyn, he thought Goldsmith was the originator. When he learned of Candy's claim for 1864 and of his use of it in games in 1866, he gave the nod to Candy.

Two other pre-1870 claimants were McSweeney of the Mutuals for 1866 and Matthews of the Lord Baltimores for 1867. The claims of the others were for the early 1870s. One such was by Alphonse ('Phoney') Martin. As an eighty-seven-year-old authority in 1932, he dropped his own claim in favor of that of Bobby Matthews. Phoney's sworn affidavit is not so much in contradiction of Candy as it is testimony that Bobby was the first spitball artist: "In 1868, I was pitching for the Eckfords and we were playing at Baltimore. Little Bobby Matthews was pitching for the Maryland lads and well do I recall the sensation he created, a revelation to all of us. Matthews would wipe one side of the ball clean, and then moisten it with the tips of his fingers and let it go. The ball would break in a wide out-curve at times and again would drop and curve in."

But in 1948, along came the late Frank W. Blair to make the case that the curveball was not of professional origin at all, but the contrivance of youngsters in Ivy League prep schools and colleges. "I have felt for many years," he wrote (in the *Amherst Graduates Quarterly*, condensed in the June, 1948, issue of *Baseball Digest*), "that professional baseball records are wrong in stating that the first curve pitching came from a professional player, Arthur Cummings." Then past ninety, he realized that "the facts in the case would never be stated unless by one of the men now living who was playing ball when curve pitching appeared."

In his dismissal of Cummings's claim, Blair said, "He was not a curve pitcher on that date [in an exhibition game with Princeton in 1874] . . . but when the ball was not in play, Cummings would take it, walk to home plate, and amaze the spectators by throwing it down to second base so it curved in its flight . . . his curve pitching came in later years."

According to Blair, Charles Hammond Avery, pitching for Yale against Harvard in 1874, was the first to pitch curves in a game of record. He, himself, Blair attests, was taught how to throw a curve in 1873 at Williston Academy by Charles Francis Carter, who had learned it from Avery. Blair, an outfielder for Williston, taught it to their pitcher, William Dennison, and thus "Williston placed on the diamond the first curve pitcher of any prep school in the country." Another of the first curvers was J. M. Mann of Princeton (1875), Blair wrote.

In an effort to end the "baseball fiction" of the origin of the curveball, Blair in 1946 sent to the Hall of Fame what he claimed was his "proof to show that the first curve pitching in baseball" was by Avery and Mann. His document is in an obscure file, while the plaque to Candy remains on public display. But Blair consoled himself: ". . . Avery, Carter, and Mann are now pitching no-hit games on a diamond in the Elysian Fields, where rain checks are never issued, pop bottles cease from troubling, and umpires are at rest." And where Mr. Blair has long since joined them.

Along with history, lore, legend, and myth, it seems likely that many inquisitive boys and men, unknown to history and each other, on real diamonds and on sandlots, behind barns and in city alleys, learned throwing techniques to deceive batters. It is true, anyway, that some of the great innovators, going back to the beginnings of baseball, are obscure to its fans.

Grover Cleveland (Old Pete) Alexander's incredible control was all the weapon he needed in the later stages of a long pitching career. He is shown here while barnstorming with the House of David team. Note the 1926 St. Louis Cardinals World Champions patch on his sweater. *The Sporting News*

If George Her-
man (Babe) Ruth
had not made the
Hall of Fame as
baseball's greatest
slugger, he would
have done so as a
curveball vir-
tuoso. But the
Babe didn't really
call his home run
shot in the 1932
World Series.
*The Sporting
News*

CHAPTER FOUR

The Birth of a Nation's Pastime

The need for the curveball to equalize the differences between safe and out grew out of the evolution of the game from loose rounders to tight baseball. Its national popularity was one of the beneficial results of the Civil War. If Abner Doubleday had invented the Civil War, as Branch Rickey joked, he could have been given an assist, at least, for making baseball our national pastime.

The best account, in my opinion, of the spread of the game to "every city, town, and hamlet" is one of the most obscure. The reminiscences of James L. (Deacon) White who, while helping spread it, became one of the most important innovators in the art of pitching, are recorded in *The Birth of a Nation's Pastime*, by Gene Kessler. It was published in 1933 and sold as a paperback for 50 cents by James Mulligan Publishing Company of St. Louis. While copies may have been guided to libraries and others may be squirreled away in attics, the

43

whereabouts of only a few copies are known. I was entrusted by Paul Mac Farlane with the one in the archives of *The Sporting News.*

It is kind of a doubleheader. It contains the complete text of the rules of baseball as set forth by Father Chadwick in 1875—still, as amended, the constitution of the game. Its treasure, though, is the gospel according to Deacon.

In 1932, Kessler went to Aurora, Illinois, to interview Jim White seven years before his death. Then eighty-five, he was the only living member of the Big Four—the first Murderer's Row—coming to bat with Jim (catcher), C. A. McVey (first base), Ross Barnes (second base), and Al Spalding (pitcher) for Boston, which won the National Association championship in 1875. An even more significant credential, historically, was that Jim was then only one of two men alive who had played baseball both before and after it became a professional sport; the other, also a Hall of Famer, was George Wright, who died in 1937 at ninety.

The Deacon (so-called "I guess because I did not bet, smoke, or drink") was introduced to baseball by a disabled Civil War veteran who organized a team in Cornish, New York, to play the game as he had learned it in the Union Army. Later, when he and Spalding were battery mates, Jim learned that Spalding, too, had been recruited into baseball by a similar disabled vet—in 1863 in Rockford, Illinois. The team Al pitched for as a kid is believed—and who is there to gainsay both Jim and Al?—to be the first real team organized "out west," as all real estate and wilderness west of the Appalachians was called by baseball folks in those days.

"So baseball is the old army game," Jim told Kessler. "Previous to the Civil War, it was played almost entirely in New York and Boston and their vicinities. Those players introduced it to the camps. The South's army learned it from captured Union soldiers. At the close of the war, soldiers of both armies carried the game to every city, town, and hamlet. In this manner, baseball was nationalized."

Jim turned pro in 1868 as captain and catcher for the Forest City Nine of Cleveland. Catching, "I stood way back and took the pitch on the first bounce. With runners on base, I stepped up behind the plate. No one wore gloves."

Studying the pitchers he caught and batted against, he began to experiment with ways to get more on the ball without violating the rules, as Jim put it, that required the pitcher "to stand flat-footed in the box and swing his arm perpendicular without bending his wrist. . . . I got my shoulder behind my heave, and my knuckles almost touched the ground" (quite like the devastating windmill pitch of present fast-pitch softball). Without a wrist-turn, his only curve was a sinking fast-ball.

In 1868, against Buffalo, with A. G.. Pratt, their regular pitcher, under the weather, Jim went to the box for the first time. "With my new wind-up delivery, I threw a faster ball than the boys had been facing, and I beat Buffalo. At Troy, Pratt was well again and pitched and lost. In New York City, the boys held a meeting and asked that I do the pitching. . . . In Brooklyn, against the Eckfords, I pitched and my wind-up motion puzzled them. We won." Then on to play the Mutuals, "the pride of Gotham, then considered the Eastern champs."

The one pitch that Jim threw against the Mutuals may well have been the most significant pitch in baseball history. In those days, the umpire was usually selected on the field before the game. The Forest City Nine had no objection to the nomination by the Mutuals of Jack Chapman, leftfielder for the Brooklyn Atlantics. After Jim's first pitch, Chapman charged out and declared it illegal. Jim argued, but Chapman told him "this is New York, not Cleveland," and kicked him out of the game. Against Pratt, the Mutuals won.

Father Chadwick, covering the game, created national controversy with his opinion that Jim's pitch was legal. Unable to prevail against a storm of disagreement, Chadwick proposed a rule change enabling the pitcher "to throw or jerk the ball to the batter with a wrist motion." His rule, adopted in 1872, legalized all deliveries "except overhand pitching and bowling as in cricket."

With the legalization of "wrist motion," both lateral and sinking curves could and did become honest deceptions.

As a catcher Jim did more to perfect the curveball than he did as a pitcher; he was a pioneer in the use of mitt and mask and was the first catcher to start an inning directly behind the plate. All of these innovations made it possible for pitchers to spin and time their curves to break at or near the plate. In addition, Jim knew how to create spin and to teach pitchers to throw curves.

Jim started to use a mitt in 1872 when he bought a large buckskin glove and put padding in it. His claim that he was the first to use a mitt is clouded by assertions of Doug Allison and Nate Hicks that they used gloves or mitts in several teams in the Independent League in 1869 and 1870.

Off-seasons at home Jim used the mitt to help his brother Bill develop and control the good curveball that gave him a successful professional career from 1875 to 1886. In 1879, Bill set the major league record for most games by pitching 75. It was in 1878, while both were playing for the Redlegs, that Jim helped his brother with a precise target by starting an inning catching from behind the plate, the first catcher to do so.

Jim became the first to use a mask in the major leagues after reading about the Man in the Iron Mask, who was catching for Harvard in 1875—Jim Tyng, whose mask was made for him by Fred Thayer, a teammate. White went out to see the mask and try it on. "It was much like a bird cage . . . too clumsy." So he got an iron worker to make a mask of steel wire. "It fit over my face with padding and was held on with an elastic band."

In 1876, with the establishment of the National League, Jim took his mitt and mask to Chicago to catch Al Spalding and help win the first National League championship. Spalding had a great but brief major league career, lasting only five years. His best year was in 1875, when Boston won the National Association championship. He pitched in 74 games with a won-lost record of 56–4, including nine shutouts.

Jim White went on to play another fourteen years in the National League, for a total professional career of twenty-two years. He played every position and wound up as a third baseman for Buffalo, Detroit, and Pittsburgh. He was in 1,278 major league games (compared with 123 for Spalding). In 5,335 at bats, he got 1,619 hits, scoring 849 runs, for a major league batting average of .303. His fielding average (as catcher, infielder, and outfielder, mostly bare-handed) was .873.

The sports writers voted Spalding into the Hall of Fame in 1939, more, one can presume, for his accomplishment in getting Cooperstown declared the birthplace than for his record as a major leaguer. The Deacon, with his record and with all he brought to the game, never made it.

But then, neither did Anthony John "the Count" Mullane, the first ambidextrous pitcher in the major leagues and one of the most versatile, expert, and popular players the game has known. Born in the County of Cork in 1859, Tony began his pro career in 1880 with Akron in the Independent League and wound it up with Toronto in the Eastern League in 1899. Along the way, including seven years with Cincinnati, he became the idol of lady fans and was one of the highest paid players of the eighties (up to $6,000). Primarily a pitcher, he also played infield and outfield and was a clutch pinch hitter. Off the diamond, he was an accomplished exhibition skater on ice and roller rinks, a clever boxer, and a musician who entertained on any instrument at hand. He was called the Count because of his "handsome dignity."

At 5' 10" and 169 pounds, Mullane was prodigiously strong. He began pitching lefthanded because, in a pregame contest at Detroit, he hurt his right arm while throwing a ball 416 feet, 7 and three-quarters inches, according to news accounts of the day. When his right arm healed, he pitched both ways. Without a glove, he would face the batter with both hands on the ball and come in with one or the other. His righthanded fastball would move up and in to a right-handed batter, who would have to be wary of an up-and-away pitch from Tony's left hand. Delivered from his set position, his pick-off throws kept runners glued to both first and third.

In 1886, he pitched 61 games, winning 31, losing 27. The next year, 1887, when batters got four strikes and walks were scored as hits, he won 31 games, including 6 shutouts, and lost 17. He pitched two doubleheaders, winning both games in 1888 and splitting in 1892. Altogether, Tony pitched 4,506 innings in 516 major league games, 466 of them complete, with 31 shutouts, 1,677 strikeouts, and a won-loss record of 285–213. Unbeguiled by his charming versatility on and off the field, the sportswriters failed to heed the pleas of his lady fans and denied him his entrance to the Hall of Fame. After quitting baseball, he became a Chicago cop. He died in 1944 at eighty-five, and lies now in Holy Sepulchre Cemetery. Like the Deacon, by the way, the Count did not bet, smoke, or drink.

Urban (Red) Faber was one of the last legal spitballers.
The Sporting News

VIRTUOSI OF THE SPITBALL

"Old Stubblebeard," Burleigh
Grimes, perhaps the greatest of all
the legal spitball pitchers. *The
Sporting News*

John Picus Quinn, one of the last legal spitballers, was forty-nine years old when he closed out his major league career in 1933. *The Sporting News*

Stan Coveleski's mastery of the spitball got him into the Hall of Fame. *The Sporting News*

As National League president and again as Commissioner of Baseball, Ford C. Frick sought in vain to make the spitball legal again. *The Sporting News*

Branch Rickey, the "Mahatma," was strongly opposed to Ford Frick's effort to legalize the spitball. *The Sporting News*

CHAPTER FIVE

Changes in the Changeless Game

Early rule changes and innovations made the curveball the essential equalizer in the balance between safe and out. The advantage the curve gave to pitchers was a fundamental consideration in further changes in rules, equipment, and the diamond to maintain defensive-offensive balance. These changes in turn begat new performing skills in the box (later the mound), at the plate, on the bases, and in the field, which begat more change and innovation. Change created new alternatives and governed changes in defensive-offensive tactics.

Before baseball was fifty years old, elements far beyond the ken of its first professionals were introduced, adapted to, and then changed. When Candy Cummings complained about the perfection of fielding in the last major league game he saw, he was not talking about greater skill but about the specialized gloves and mitts that made the impossible plays of his day routine fifty years later.

As Jim White put it: "In my day fielding was better. We had to handle the ball bare-handed, which requires greater skill. But today's pitching and batting are so far advanced there is no comparison." Tony Mullane's ambidexterous pitching and pick-off throws would not have been possible with a glove on one hand.

Change continues. Greater change, beyond our ken, is sure to come. No aspect of baseball is simple. The effect of change upon the game as it is played and upon the lives and careers of the professionals who play it is more complex than is generally perceived, and cannot reliably be predicted.

Change has made valid comparisons impossible between players of one era and another. It is less obvious, however, that many accepted comparisons between the American and National leagues—or between one major league season and the next—are disputable because of the kind and amount of change in each. The designated hitter (a nonfielding player who bats instead of the pitcher), in use in the American League but still against the law in the National League, affects batting and pitching performances—and the careers of batters and pitchers—differently and profoundly. Differences in the height of the pitching mound and in the size of the strike zone from one season to the next affect both batting and pitching performances, as we shall see.

And yet, as baseball is always changing, its essence never changes—a paradox that is one of its greatest fascinations. When one looks at long-ago and recent changes in the game—in the ball, bat, gloves and mitts, and other equipment (the innovation of the batting helmet!); in pitching distance and rules; in size, shape, surfaces, lighting, and the air of ball parks and stadiums; in salaries and life-styles of players and in the opportunity to play in the major leagues—the changeless essence of baseball seems to parallel the changeless human spirit as it endures the long ages of change in the human condition.

As we look at change in baseball, we see that one unchanging feature is the way its professional players have exploited, mitigated, and circumvented changes in rules and conditions in order to succeed, or just to survive, in merciless competition. To stay in the majors for substantial careers, players must adjust to changes in themselves as well as in the game. They must compensate with craft and savvy for loss of agility, power, and speed, as age, fatigue, and injury beset muscle and bone. Those who do are sensitive to every advantage, however small, within or outside the law, that they can perceive, discover, or devise.

The nature of the baseball itself is the main reason why only the most guileful curveball pitchers can perform successfully in the major leagues for very long after their physical prime and on into middle age. Though balls, as we have seen, are now made the same way, of the same materials in the same factory, for both leagues, no two are exactly alike. (Place two or three balls on a flat surface and watch how each rolls its own way to equilibrium.) The tiny differences in circumference, weight, irregularity of seams, and smoothness of surfaces are exploited by sensitive pitchers to enhance curves and create greater aberration in the flight of spinless pitches. Since the dawn of the game, pitchers have supplemented inherent irregularities with those of their own devising. Their ability to take advantage of differences in apparently identical balls is one reason why so many curveball and spinless ball pitchers have such high market value and long careers.

Through the years there have been many actual and suspected changes in the "liveliness" and "deadness" of the ball. In manufacture, the quality and tightness of yarn wound around a cork or rubber center and the tightness of its leather cover—now of cowhide, not horsehide—has changed the premium skills of the game from offensive to defensive, back and forth. This was done, no doubt about it, by influential owners, both to give greater advantage to their teams' style of play and to sell more tickets to their games.

Though nowadays there is no evidence of season-to-season changes in manufacturing resilience, players and sportswriters and fans are quick to attribute an unusual spate of homers to a more lively ball, in ignorance of more likely factors. Such was the case in the early going of the 1983 season, when even banjo hitters were knocking the ball over the walls in the widespread and unusually rainy, low-pressure weather, in which batted balls sailed up and far.

Almost all the significant changes in the bat were made in the early years. In their search for tough, seasoned wood, manufacturers advertised for old wagon tongues, and many bats were hewn from them. ("Swing that ol' wagon tongue up there!") In 1880, when maximum diameter was 2½ inches and length was 42 inches, a four-sided bat was permitted, but this batter advantage was taken back the next year and roundness restored. Briefly, though, in the mid-eighties, the rules declared that "a portion of the bat may be flat on one side." Taping the handle or applying a "granulated substance" up to 18 inches from the end was permitted to tighten grips, an advantage to batters, and to protect the innocent from sweat-slick flying missiles.

The most commonly used "granulated substance" is good old sticky pine tar, which, on George Brett's bat, created one of the most controversial applications and interpretations of the rule since it has been in the book. On Sunday, July 24, 1983, playing in New York against the Yankees, Brett hit a two-run homer in the ninth that put the Kansas City Royals ahead, 5–4. Billy Martin, Yankee manager, and his coaches, who had spotted tar more than 18 inches up the handle on Brett's bat, immediately protested the use of what they contended was an illegal bat. Measuring, the umpires found the conspicuous tar applied too high up. They disallowed the runs and called Brett out. On appeal by the Royals, however, Lee McPhail, president of the American League, reversed his umpires and restored the two runs, ruling that the Royals were leading, 5–4; if necessary to determine divisional championship, the game would be continued with two out in the top of the ninth. (Which ultimately it was, without further incident and with the 5–4 score holding up.) Most knowledgeable baseball people agreed that Brett did not swing an illegal bat—one that was scored, hollowed, plugged, leaded, or covered with anything invisible that would have doctored the contact surface—but merely one that did not meet regulations, and that the umpires should have removed the bat from the game before it was used. The Yankees should have protested its use before, not after, the homer.

In the 1890s the whiplike flexibility of willow—("Swing that ol' willow up there!")—was outlawed by a decree that bats must be made of hard wood with a maximum diameter of 2¾ inches. The only two rule changes affecting bats in this century came in 1939, when laminated bats were banned, and in 1954, when the ban was modified to permit submission of laminated bats for approval, which hasn't happened. The ping of aluminum bats heard in softball and amateur and college baseball has not replaced the crack of the bat in professional baseball. So bats are pretty much as they were when hewn from wagon tongues, a source that has dried up.

The permitted enlargement of mitts and gloves and their pocket areas has blessed pitchers. A catcher's mitt of up to 38 inches in circumference makes catching a knuckleball merely difficult instead of impossible. The permitted 13-inch length of gloves, and development of enlarged pockets, have turned countless hits into pretty outs.

Though the term remains idiomatic in baseball, business, and courtship, no one has been "knocked out of the box" in this century. The old pitchers box, moved back five feet in 1881 to 50 feet and still another five feet a year later (to give batters a better chance against such fastballers as Amos Rusie), was replaced in 1883 with a rubber slab, 12 by 4 inches, on a mound of unspecified height 60 feet 6 inches from the plate, which has remained the pitching distance ever since.

In the "game of inches," perhaps the most important inches are the height of the mound. It was set at 15 inches in 1904 and there it remained for sixty-five years, until in 1969 it was lowered to 10 inches, a tremendous advantage to batters. Before calculating the effect of lowering the mound, though, we must include the effects of changes in the strike zone. A called strike was a pitch over the plate and between the batter's armpits and the top of his knees until 1963, when the strike zone was expanded, to the pitcher's advantage, to the top of the shoulder and the bottom of the knee. But then—nothing in baseball, remember, is simple—when the mound was lowered five inches in 1969 for one batter advantage, the strike zone was shortened back to armpits and top of knee for another.

Tom Shieber, a young fan and neighbor of mine in St. Louis, looked up and calculated the effects of changes in the height of the mound and size of the strike zone on batting. In 1968, with the 15-inch mound, 1,104 home runs were belted in the American League, one for every 49 at-bats; and 891 in the National, one for every 62, a major league total of 1,995 home runs. In 1969, with the 10-inch mound, the American League hit 1,649, 1 for 40, 345 more than from the 15-incher; the National League total in 1969 went way up to 1,470, 1 for 45 and 579 more; thus there was a total for both leagues of 924 more homers—an increase of 46 percent. This amounts to 184.8 more homers for each inch the mound was lowered. (Lowering the mound seems to have taken more off the curves and sinkers of the National League, the traditional home of such pitches, than off the action of American League fastball pitches.)

To check the probable effect of the tighter strike zone, Tom compared home run production in 1963 (armpits to top of knee) with 1962 (top of shoulder to bottom of knee), both from the 15-inch mound. By being allowed to lay off lower and higher pitches in 1963, batters of both leagues hit 2,604 homers, 603 more than the year before—an increase of 23 percent. To play the numbers game and factor out the advantage of a tighter strike zone to batters, it can be concluded that lowering the mound five inches increased home run production by nearly 25 percent, or about 5 percent an inch.

The extent to which pitchers have been able to adjust their deliveries and stuff, especially action pitches, to the lower mound is, statistically, complicated by such yet unmeasurable factors as league expansion (dilution of talent), playing conditions in the new ballparks, the emergence of relief specialists, and so on, with all their advantages and disadvantages for batters, pitchers, and fielders. But pitching remains the deciding factor in most games and all pennant races.

The effects of the designated hitter in the American League are not simple, either. It was assumed, and is widely believed, that giving long-ball hitting specialists some 12,000 at-bats a season, in place of weak-hitting pitchers, would increase the American League's traditional lead in home runs over the National League. But that hasn't happened. In 1973, the first year of the designated hitter, there were 1,552 home runs in the American League and 1,550 in the National—one for every 43 at-bats in both leagues. Since then, the American League has hit about as many more per season than the National as it did before the designated hitter, but the margin has not increased.

One effect of the D.H. rule is that there are more complete games pitched in the American League, since pitchers are not taken out for pinch hitters. And, say foes of the designated hitter, more sore arms and shortened pitching careers result from leaving them in. The familiar and heated arguments for and against the designated hitter do not seem to be changing minds in either entrenchment. It may well be, though, that the widespread use of the designated hitter in lower levels of the game (including college ball) constitutes an ominous trend for the tactical purists of the National League. Meanwhile, undeniably their role as designated hitters is giving heroic employment to many old sluggers who otherwise would have gone home.

The pros and cons of the artificial surface, while changing the talents of the game, are pretty much a standoff in terms of hits and outs. Shots streaking past infielders for hits are canceled by others that could have been legged out for hits on a slower infield. One change is in the kind of ability that is required on artificial playing surfaces; a quick acrobat like Ozzie Smith is needed instead of the angular range and sureness of Marty Marion, the Mr. Shortstop of his day on the grass. Another is that fewer games are called or postponed because of rain and wet grounds, which means fewer make-up doubleheaders and less strain on a pitching staff in the season-long run for the money.

There is also the difference between night and day. The big advantage that night ball gave to pitchers becomes smaller as ballpark lights get better. The contrast between sunlight and shade makes pitching, batting, and fielding trickier in the old ballparks. A pitcher throwing from sunshine at a plate in shade knows that his curve or fastball is going to seem to disappear in the deep purple shade. But as the shadows move out to the edge of the mound, the pitcher begins to feel like a vaudeville magician in a blinding spotlight; the spin of the earth has given the advantage to the poised batter waiting to see what this pitcher is going to try to put over on him. There were tough sunfields in all the old ballparks, each different in April and September and each from the others. But players adjusted or went home, just as they did to night ball and as they adapted their rhythms of work and rest from a game followed by an overnight berth in a Pullman to a pillow on a jet and a hotel bed a thousand miles away at three in the morning.

In the high-tiered stadiums that began replacing the old ballparks, outside wind speed and direction are distorted by inside stillness, shifting gusts, or sudden turbulence. (Often in St. Louis's Busch Stadium, when it is converted to football, the four endzone flags near ground level are flying in different directions, while Old Glory up above is undulating in a steady northwest wind.) What kind of a pitch do you throw and where do you aim it if you don't know which way the wind will take it after you throw it?

Now the trend is to domed stadiums that create new kinds of change for everybody. The all-weather comfort to fans, and the elimination of the nuisance of rain delays and the disappointment of planning and making a long trek to see a game only to find it postponed, may have an effect on the intensity and caliber of the play of the game. Are the well-dressed spectators in an on-the-town mood in the well-appointed Astrodome in Houston more, or less, inspiring or annoying to the players than the raucous, half-naked fans in the bleachers at old Wrigley Field?

Spectators aside, Joe Niekro of the Astros believes that the stable cool air under the rigid dome will add three years to his pitching career, because he can throw his knuckleball, curves, and fastball with confidence that he, not changes in the air, is in charge of their whimsicalities. The cooled air under rigid domes, sinking with its weight, would seem, aerodynamically, to hold up the flight and velocity of thrown and batted balls and provide a more favorable climate for curveballs than fastballs. In 1964, the Houston players and their opponents hit 73 home runs in the old open ballpark; the next year, under the dome, they hit only 57, but then, the fences were further back.

To whatever extent the descending cool air under rigid domes affects the play of the game, it could not be the same as the effect of the air that holds up the flexible dome in the non-air-conditioned Metrodome in Minneapolis. Again, there are too many variables, including the quality of players, to sift out the statistical effect, but the up-lifting air may have been the main reason that the Twins had a team batting average of .229 in 1981 in the open air at home, and one of .268 the next year under their balloonlike dome. Until more is known, pitchers might be well advised to put more reliance for key outs on fastballs than on curveballs when pitching in the Metrodome.

One of the biggest and most measurable changes in baseball is in dollars—those that go into the investment portfolios of star players, into decent salaries for average players, into the complex financial jungles of corporate and individual owners, and, every dollar of it, out of the pockets of fans.

In the last thirty years, with the advent of free agency, television income, and bigger stadiums, bench warmers are now making three times more than stars formerly were paid, and the take of stars is up a hundredfold (compare the salary of Dizzy Dean with that of Steve Carlton, for example). Because the bookkeeping of owners is mysterious and devious, their take—including tax concessions, shelters, and write-offs—is known only to them (but not to each other) and, if He is interested, to God.

The only good and interesting case that anyone in this favored land of Me-Tooism can make against decent salaries for average players (a minimum wage of $35,000 a year) and even against the astronomical star contracts must be based on (a) how they affect quality of play and (b) the cost of enjoying baseball. Do million-dollar contracts and the hope for them inspire better play, or create pressures that choke it?

The million-dollar batter grounds into a game-ending double play. The fans groan: "He ain't worth what he's makin'." Do the boos in his ears create doubt in his mind? Pridefully, he tries harder and gets tenser and slumps further below the batting average and home run production he is expected to deliver. "All that bum cares about is the dough he's banking."

The pitcher may be getting paid $1,000 a pitch. How much for the flat slider he throws that costs a pennant?

How do dollars affect the chance-taking of the play? A $35,000-per-year Pete Reiser got knots on his head slamming against outfield walls, pursued by one obsession only—catch the ball! Does not the million-dollar property have a responsibility to think twice before making a "hospital try"?

Do the big bucks affect the quality of play, or merely the expectations of fans? Can the million-dollar star ever be the kind of hero that Pete Reiser was?

And how about dollars and drugs? Long before John L. Sullivan hit the skids by quaffing Black Velvet (champagne and stout) from the slippers of chorus girls, the ruination of poor boys who suddenly had money in every pocket has been a sad story in professional sports. In addition to the traditional excesses of booze, broads, fancy shirts and collars, and so forth, some of today's successful athletes smoke, swallow, snort, or shoot dope. Some fall into it by rising up to an expensive high style. It's the thing to do, and they've got the money to do the thing. So do folks of the jet set and other flights of stylish life.

For others, more insidiously, it is the greenies ("mother's little helper" of the suburbs) they pop to get up for competitive performance, and the downers or tranks they swallow afterwards with a few beers to relax. The notion that hooks them is: "With the money I'm making, I've got to get the job done every day." This desperate accommodation of pressure in the struggle for survival and success is scarcely unique to the few overpaid ballplayers who stumble and fall.

It is not player salaries alone that make going to a ball game an expensive adventure. When we were living in New York in the Pete Reiser era, Margaret and I went to Ebbets Field (or to the Polo Grounds or Yankee Stadium) by subway for a nickel. The best available box or grandstand seat cost no more than $2.50. Two beers for me and a lemonade for her came to 95 cents, three hot dogs and a bag of peanuts meant another buck. With what was left of $10, we could drink martinis and argue the game's decisions with the other trolley dodgers (hence the name Brooklyn Dodgers) in the bar and grill on the corner.

Today a similar excursion to Busch Stadium (by car—how else?) costs $30, not including the martinis. Bring along a couple of kids (and pay a babysitter for the little one at home), and a family can easily spend $50 to go out to the new ballpark.

Watching at home on television is paid for by those whose choice of beer, cars, insurance, chewing gum, and soap is influenced by the commercials. Whatever its other joys and aggravations, television coverage—a zoom lens in dead centerfield—gives the fan at home a better look at the pitching action than any fan at the park has ever enjoyed, a view that only the game pitchers themselves had before television.

Through and after all the changes in the game, its verities remain. "It ain't over till it's over," however long that may take. Ungoaded by seconds left on the clock, unconcerned with frantic efforts to stop their ticking away, a baseball game proceeds at its own sweet pace, punctuated by reflexive response to instantaneous decision, until its final out.

It is a game played alone on a team. Depending upon synchrony of teamwork, each player succeeds or fails in his role all by himself. The shortstop is all alone diving to knock the ball down and shovel it to the covering second baseman, who makes a throw at the top of his lonely leap over the take-out slide of the runner to the solitary, stretching first baseman—just another 6–4–3 double play in the history of the game.

Every pitch and play is seen, judged, and recorded. As fans, alone in a crowd, we can see and judge the judgment.

Baseball's basic skills—never mind the changes to which players must adjust—are eternal. Cool Papa Bell, who helped Jackie Robinson break the color line, the most important change in the history of the game, said about the way it is and the way it was in his time, outside the pale: "There's nothin' the same except the game." And as Lou Brock, not yet eligible for the Hall of Fame to which Cool Papa was named in 1974, said after the two great base stealers got together: "It is interesting that our theories on running are so similar. There are some things about baseball that will never change. That's why it's such a fascinating game."

BASEBALL GRIPS

Palm ball, just before release, when thumb would open to minimize downspin, as demonstrated by Andy Coakley, longtime major leaguer and Columbia University coach.

Ed Walsh's spitter grip. Note fingers and thumb are on smooth surface. If thumb is positioned on seam, more downspin is created. Walsh won 39 games for the White Sox in 1908.

Classic forkball grip as demonstrated by Pete Stanridge of the Cubs and Cardinals.

The knuckler, as thrown by Ed Cicotte.

Because Frank Shellenback's name was omitted from the list of those allowed to continue throwing the spitball in the majors after 1919, he spent two decades as a top-flight pitcher in the Pacific Coast League. *The Sporting News*

Tommy Bridges of the Detroit Tigers was small, and a master of the curveball and, 'tis said, the wet one.
The Sporting News

The all-time king of the screwball, Carl Owen Hubbell of the Giants. With that pitch he fanned, in succession, Babe Ruth, Lou Gehrig, Jimmy Foxx, Al Simmons, and Joe Cronin in the 1934 All-Star game.
The Sporting News

Carl Hubbell threw screwballs with such regularity for the New York Giants that his left wrist was turned permanently inward. Left to right, Bill Lohrman, Harry Gumbert, Cliff Melton, and Hubbell. *The Sporting News*

Had Paul (Daffy) Dean, at left, been able to supplement his fastball with a decent curve, many believe he might have surpassed the pitching feats of his brother Jerome (Dizzy) Dean. Photograph taken in 1934, when between them the Dean brothers won 49 regular season and 4 World Series games for the St. Louis Cardinals. *The Sporting News*

CHAPTER SIX

Why the Fastball Needs the Curve

Though he could not cite chapter and verse, my father believed and taught me that God so loved baseball that He created man with a frail arm unsuited to long stints of power pitching. Thus did He assure development of a game of hard choices in which great success and bare survival alike depend upon native cunning and practiced skills.

As a catcher in semipro ball in St. Louis around the turn of the century and as a dedicated fan, my dad was a wise judge of baseball flesh. As I neared sixteen and aspired to move up as a pitcher from sandlot to American Legion ball, he was catching my best stuff with a fielder's glove when he analyzed my prospects:

"Son, God did not give you a good fastball. He was miserly with them. Even those who got good ones had to mix them with curves and change-ups and funny balls to be great or even good major league pitchers." He paused. "Except for one man." I knew who—Big Barney, the Big Train himself. "The others," he went on, "had to learn to set up their fastballs with nickel curves, full curves, knuckleballs, forkballs, spitballs, slippery elm balls, shine balls, emery balls, scuffed balls, cut balls, mud balls, needle balls, raised seam balls, frozen balls— whatever they could best adapt to their fingers, wrists, and elbows to keep those batters off-balance at the plate, inning after inning, game after game, season after season. Now if you want to be a pitcher in tough competition, son, you've got no choice but to learn and practice control of curves and funny balls."

"But, Dad," I said, being also the son of my mother, "most of those pitches ain't legal any more."

"That," he said, "is for you to know and them to find out."

My father's wisdom served me well enough in the amateur ball of which I was capable, but it was years later before I appreciated the fundamental baseball truth of what he told me.

In 1955, Arthur Daley of the *New York Times*, who thought knowledgeably and wrote well about the charms of baseball, was musing about the fastball. "The blazer," he concluded, "is God-given. A pitcher can be taught curves, sliders, and fancy didoes, but the fastball cannot be acquired."

Major League scouts are always on the lookout for youngsters with the gift, and they identify and sign quite a few in the expectation that the kids will acquire a curve mixture to make their fastballs devastating. One reason so few of them make it to the majors permanently is that their fastballs are so effective in the minor leagues that they get the notion that pure power is all they need. In the majors, it is not enough.

A sad example is Karl Spooner, a lefthanded fastballer who was brought up by the Dodgers toward the end of the 1954 season. The records he set with his smoke made him look like a new Lefty Grove— fifteen strikeouts in his first major league game, including six in a row; his first two major league games were shutouts in which he struck out a total of twenty-seven batters. The next year, though, with major league batters anticipating and timing his fastball without curves to worry about, his arm gave out as he won eight games, lost six, and was through.

A good many pure power pitchers had remarkable but all too brief major league careers. Rex Barney of the Dodgers probably threw as hard as anybody. They said he could throw a ball through a brick wall if he could hit the wall. Another fastballer, Ryne Duren, was, briefly, a brilliant reliever for the Yankees in the late fifties because of the intimidation that his uncertain control gave him over batters. Coming in for his warm-up pitches, he would peer down at his catcher through glasses so thick they looked, as someone said, like the bottoms of Coke bottles, and blaze a pitch into the screen. This would give the batter first and second thoughts about survival, before, thirdly, he would think about hitting Duren's fastballs. Before his arm gave out, Duren fanned thirty batters in one stretch of twenty innings in relief. Ten years earlier Joe Page had a brilliant and brief career as a fastballing reliever for the Yankees.

Every fan can name other fastball pitchers—the likes of Bob Turley, Don Ferrarese, Leo Kiely, Von McDaniel, Clint Hartung, and Paul Dean come at random to mind—whose pure power did not last through long careers. Many baseball people believe that if Paul Dean had developed a curveball, especially a slider, before he threw his arm out, he would have gone on to win ranking among the greatest pitchers.

Most of the great fastballers came up with some combination of curve, change-up, and control to keep batters guessing as they threw smoke past them in what proved to be significantly long careers. Surging at random through an old fan's memories are the names of Robin Roberts, Sandy Koufax, Juan Marichal, Sad Sam Jones, Bob Gibson, Allie Reynolds, Whitey Ford, Rube Waddell, Rick Gossage, Steve Carlton, Tom Seaver, Ron Guidry, Sam McDowell, and the two Dons, Newcombe and Drysdale. Feel free to add your favorites. We'll hear about some of these versatile pitchers when we look at the curves and crooked pitches they judiciously mixed with their fastballs.

We will also see how Christy Mathewson, Ol' Pete Alexander, Satchel Paige (in his twilight), and others developed the "something else" that made their ordinary fastballs into effective "out" pitches. But some of the very greatest pitchers came up to the major leagues with extraordinary fastballs that would not for long have been enough without the wicked curves they learned to throw.

I include Nolan Ryan in this category, though he is marginal because he was not ignorant of the deception of the curve when he came up. Ryan relied almost entirely on power until he began increasingly to reduce strain on his arm and expand the unhittability of his fastball with a good curve and surprising change-ups. In May of the 1983 season, at thirty-six, he pitched his 3,509th strikeout, one more than Walter Johnson's longstanding record. Since then, Steve Carlton's slider has put Johnson in third place. With both Ryan and Carlton still going strong, there is no way to be sure which will end up as King of Strike-outs. Meanwhile, there is no contender in sight to challenge Ryan's record of five no-hitters. Furthermore, it is calculated that the Houston Astros are paying him about $10,000 an hour for his time spent on the mound.

Perhaps the greatest of all pitchers to learn the curve midway in his career as a fastballer was Denton (Cy) Young, who pitched in both major leagues from 1890 until 1911. He came up with Cleveland at twenty-three and won 193 games with pure power and only fair control. Then, in 1897, he added a curve and sharpened his control. By the time he hung it up, he had won 511 games, the most ever, and pitched 906 games (topped by Hoyt Wilhelm's 1,070, but Hoyt's were mostly in relief, while Cy started and finished almost all of his games).

Bob Feller was another. He came up with Cleveland in 1936 as a seventeen-year-old fireballer. With an uncompromising fastball, he won 107 games in the next five years, including a no-hitter against the White Sox in the opening game of the 1940 season. Then he gave three and a half years of wartime service to the Navy and came back to baseball a better pitcher—with a wide curve and a quick slider to go with his still formidable fastball. In the next ten years he pitched two more no-hitters and twelve one-hitters while racking up a total of 266 wins and 2,581 strikeouts, all for the Indians.

During his five years with the Baltimore Orioles of the International League, Bob (Lefty) Grove won 109 games with fastballs. Coming up with the Philadelphia Athletics in 1925, he continued winning without a curve. His fastball career reached its zenith in 1928 when, on August 23 and again on September 27, he struck out three consecutive batters on nine pitches, the only major league pitcher to do it twice. Then he began to throw a curve. With it, at thirty in 1930, he won 28 games for the Athletics, and 31 more, losing only four, the next year. He won four World Series games, two in 1930 and two in 1931, both against the Cardinals, with an earned-run average of only 1.75. Traded to the Boston Red Sox in 1934, he pitched for another eight years, retiring at forty-one with an even 300 major league victories and an earned-run average of 3.06.

Arthur (Dazzy) Vance used the ten best years of his right arm throwing fastballs in the minor leagues before he was called up by the Brooklyn Dodgers in 1922, when he was thirty-one years old. Learning the wisdom and mechanics of the curve, he pitched for fourteen years in the major leagues, mostly for the Dodgers. He led the league in strikeouts for seven years. He was forty-four when he retired after the 1935 season. He won 197 games in the major leagues using the curveball, and 133 in the minors without it.

Perhaps the most gallant effort to prolong a major league career by throwing curves was that of Jay (Dizzy) Dean. As a demon fastball pitcher with the St. Louis Cardinals, winning 30 games and losing 7 with 195 strikeouts and an earned-run average of 2.65 in 1934, he "fogged 'em past 'em" until the All-Star game of 1937, when a shot off the bat of Earl Averill, the slugging outfielder of the Cleveland Indians, hit him in the foot and knocked him out of the box as a supreme fastball pitcher.

The Chicago Cubs, though, gambled on his recovery by giving $185,000 and three players for him as the 1938 season began. With his fastball "nothin' but a melon," he threw an astonishing assortment of curves and slow stuff off his gimpy foot, winning seven and losing only one as the Cubs won the National League pennant. Against the New York Yankees of 1938 ("the greatest ball club ever assembled," in the opinion of their manager, Marse Joe McCarthy), Dizzy was called upon to pitch the second game of the World Series. For seven innings he held the mighty Yankees to two runs with, as he said later, "a big windmill motion and throwing off-speed balls." In the eighth inning, with Dean's arm in pain "as if bone was sticking out of the flesh," Frank Crosetti came to bat with one on and one out. With a two-ball and two-strike count, Ol' Diz got a junky curve past Frank for what he thought was strike three, but the umpire called it ball three. Crosetti whacked the next pitch into the stands, and that was it for Dean, though he hung around for a couple of years and pitched exhibition ball in the sticks where folks remembered the glory of his fastball.

The opinion of many that of all pitchers endowed with the fastball only the Big Train, Walter (Barney) Johnson, was able to mow batters down with it over a long career without an offsetting curve could be disputed by those who bring up Amos Rusie. Rusie's velocity and intimidation of batters in the early nineties was the main consideration in the decision to move the mound back to 60 feet, 6 inches in 1893. In 1890 he had won 29 games and struck out 345 batters pitching for the New York Giants. The next year he won 32, including a no-hitter against Brooklyn, and struck out 321. The extra five feet given the batters did not help them much against his blazer. In each of eight seasons he won 20 or more games, including 36 in 1894, for the Giants.

But his major league career lasted only ten seasons, including a final feeble stint with the Cincinnati Redlegs, who traded Christy Mathewson to get him, in which he allowed 25 hits and 15 runs in the three games he worked and did not win any of them. And so we come back to Johnson, who was not in the same class with other fastball pitchers. He was in a class by himself.

"Stee-rike!" the umpire called Johnson's pitch as the long shadows turned to dusk at Griffith Stadium.

The batter disagreed. "That sounded low," he said and headed for the dugout.

"That's only two," the umpire called after him. "You've got another strike coming."

"Take it yourself," the batter told him.

The next batter came to the plate carrying a brakeman's lantern.

"Do you think," said the umpire with a sneer, "that's going to help you see the ball?"

"I ain't worried about that," the batter said. "I just want to make sure the Big Train can see me."

Those stories were vouched for as true by players of Johnson's time, 1907 through 1927, with the Senators, a team that was known as "Washington—first in war, first in peace, and last in the American League." Without resorting to the trickery of curves or funny balls in those twenty-one years, he pitched 816 games and won 416, both the most ever in the American League. On September 4, 5, and 7 in 1908, he pitched successive complete game shutouts, a record never surpassed. In 1912, from July 3 to August 23, he won 16 successive games, tying the American League record.

And he did it all with fastballs, and in daylight! Nick Altrock, a contemporary pitcher who achieved fame also as a baseball comedian, was not just joking when he said that if Johnson had pitched night ball, Congress would have had to pass a law against him.

George Sisler, one of the very best hitters and first basemen ever to play the game and who, as a St. Louis Brown, batted against Johnson many times, said, long after both their careers were in the books: "I've often wondered what kind of record Johnson would have had if he'd had a curve or a spitter or some other fancy pitches to mix in with his fastball. I've come to one inescapable conclusion. No one ever would have gotten a hit off him. Every game he pitched would have been a no-hitter."

Though Johnson fooled around with a curve toward the end of his career, it was never a factor in his record. Nor did he throw tight to keep batters loose. The fear was in Johnson that he would hit a batter with his fastball. Knowing of Johnson's concern, mean and crafty Ty Cobb would crowd the plate against him, and, sure enough, Johnson would ease up or pitch away from him. Nor did Johnson throw any of the doctored balls, even when they were legal. He probably could not have controlled them, anyway. Once when an infielder scuffed a ball before returning it, Johnson's next pitch sailed over the catcher's head, high against the backstop.

It was not his size or unusual strength that gave his pitches their velocity and action. He was a big guy for his time, 6'1" and 210 pounds, but there have been bigger and stronger pitchers who did not have his stuff. He did have unusually long arms, but it was the tireless motion of every coordinated muscle that seemed to make the ball become a living thing. His momentum at release carried him a peculiar little jump forward. Righthanded, he threw just a little above sidearm and released the ball with a snap (not a turn) of his wrist that increased both the velocity and spin of the ball. The spin (counterclockwise) caused the ball to curve, or arc, up and in to a righthanded batter.

Yes, a spinning fastball does curve; or, as they say, it "moves" or "sails" or "sinks," depending upon the amount and direction of its rotation. As the studies of Dr. Briggs confirmed, the amount of curve depends upon the RPM of the ball, not its velocity. The spin of the fastball, achieved without wrist-turn, does not have the RPM of a true curve, which results from finger pressure and wrist-turn and causes the ball to spin the other way (clockwise from a righthander). The wrist-turn, while increasing a reverse and causing greater spin, also reduces velocity. The fastball does not curve as much or as suddenly, but comes in with undiminished velocity.

Writing in the Baltimore *Sun*, Bob Maisel recalled in 1983 how his father, Fritz, a Yankee opponent of Johnson, described the master's fastball: "He would bring it around almost like slow motion, and then right at the point of delivery, he would snap that wrist and the ball would seem to explode. It would seem to rise about a foot, a rising ball in the strike zone."

Some pitchers, like Bob Gibson of the Cardinals, can make their fastballs sail or sink. Bob gripped his sailer with his first and second finger across the seam, making the ball spin back toward him, or up to the batter. He gripped the sinker on the smooth surface; his thumb and third fingers on the bottom seam created downspin without loss of velocity.

While it was the most common pitch before 1884 when overhand pitching was permitted, the underhand fastball has been, and still is, effective for a few pitchers. After he hurt his shoulder playing football at Kansas State, Elden Auker could not throw hard overhanded. The underhand pitching motion he developed—the submarine ball—gave him several good years with the St. Louis Browns in the thirties. "When I throw it as a fastball, it rises and sinks," he said of it. "When I turn my wrist, it rises as it breaks." In the fifties, Ted Abernathy also threw both the rainbow drop fastball and the curving upshoot. The best known of contemporary underhanded fastballers are the relief specialists Dan Quisenberry of the Royals and Kent Tekulve of the Pirates. The main advantage of this exotic fastball is its unfamiliarity to batters; its disadvantage is that an offsetting curve from the same motion is an armkiller.

Johnson's fastball was once timed at 127 feet per second, but that was more a measure of the slow thumb of the timer than of his pitch's velocity. Had he been timed by modern devices, there can be no doubt his velocity would have been at least as great as Feller's (98.6 MPH) and perhaps, like Ryan's, in the 100-plus MPH range.

Johnson, born in 1887, was brought up in Coffeyville, Kansas, the hometown of another great fastballer, Frank (Red Ant) Wickware. Some said Red Ant was faster and a much more clever pitcher than Johnson. But, like those of so many other great black ballplayers of his era, his record comes to us only as legend. You can't look it up.

The Big Train, inducted into the Hall of Fame in 1936, ten years before his death, needed only his God-given fastball to achieve baseball immortality. Everybody else has had to learn to throw curves and funny balls.

Thirty-nine-year-old Fred Fitzsimmons, of Brooklyn, demonstrating his knuckleball grip to young Marius Russo of the New York Yankees, shut out the Bronx Bombers for six innings in the 1941 World Series until a line drive broke his kneecap, and Russo went on to beat the Dodgers, 2–1. *The Sporting News*

Bob Feller in his youthful strength, in 1940. Neither his fourth nor little finger tips are touching the ball as he prepares to throw the fast one that he relied upon most of the time until after World War II. *The Sporting News*

Feller's fastball was clocked at 98.6 MPH in this 1946 test. *The Sporting News*

Ty Cobb and Stan (The Man) Musial in 1952. Musial once said of the lighting in a minor league ballpark that "I couldn't see which way the ball was spinning until it was half-way on me." *The Sporting News*

Four knuckleballers made up the wartime Washington Senators' starting rotation in 1945. Demonstrating their differing grips, left to right, are Johnny Niggeling, Roger Wolff, Emil Leonard, and Mickey Haefner. *The Sporting News*

Truett (Rip) Sewell demonstrates the release of his famed blooper, or "eephus ball." *William C. Greene*

Ted Williams of the Boston Red Sox when he was truly the "splendid splinter." Ted's second home run in the 1947 All-Star game was the only homer ever hit off Rip Sewell's "eephus ball." *The Sporting News*

CHAPTER SEVEN

The Deuce You Say

The Boston Red Sox, reviewing their pitching tactics against the New York Yankees, came to consider Joe Di-Maggio. "Pitch him curves," said Joe McCarthy, then, in 1948, in his first year of managing Boston after fifteen years at the Yankee helm. Birdie Tebbetts, a thinking catcher who later became an astute manager, presumed to differ: "We've been pitching him fastballs. He's a good curveball hitter."

"Young man," said Marse Joe, "there are no good curveball hitters."

This is because there is no such thing, really, as *a* curveball. Like the balls themselves, every curve is different—even those thrown by the same pitcher the same way in the same inning with the same ball to the same batter. It is impossible to throw two identical curves. While pitches of one kind of curve behave pretty much alike, they vary in

81

velocity, break, and point of arrival in or out of the strike zone. In addition to their individual personalities, curves come in as many varieties as pickles.

They can, however, be divided into two main groups—legal and illegal. I think of curves as a clan of honest respectable folk in the bottoms who have outlaw cousins up in the hills. It is well to introduce friends to the former before taking them up to enjoy the crooked doings of the latter. That's what we'll do here.

In describing the different kinds of curves and how they come in to the batter, I find the terminology of my youth more vivid than current changing jargon. The old-fashioned nomenclature, as I use it, applies to righthanded pitches thrown to righthanded batters. What is out and away from a righthanded batter is in and on a lefthander. Lefthanded pitches spin and curve the other way.

Beginning with the clockwise spinning fastballs, an overhand fastball, rising as it nears the batter, is an "upshoot." The "inshoot," thrown sidearm, curves toward him. The "drop," or "rainbow drop," curves down. The ball "moves," as they now say, with the angle of the arm, from straight up to straight down, at release. How much it moves depends upon how fast it is spinning, which varies from pitcher to pitcher and from pitch to pitch, with grip, finger strength, motion, air conditions, and intention, as well as other factors of which neither the batter nor the pitcher himself may be aware, including what each thinks the other may be expecting in the game situation.

The basic true curves, spinning counterclockwise, are the overhand "drop," the three-quarter-arm "outdrop," the sidearm "out," and the underhand "rise ball." The clockwise spinning curve, achieved by turning the wrist the other way, to the inside instead of the outside, has for long been known as the screwball, except by Christy Mathewson, who called it his fadeaway. With all spinning curves, the amount of break and when and where they break and their velocity depend, like almost everything else in baseball, upon an infinitude of factors.

The spinless curves, which are intended to fly erratically in their airstreams, get their names from the grips and motions that create them—the knuckleball, forkball (when not thrown with "drop" spin), palm ball, slip ball, etc. Spinless curves, however gripped, are thrown with fastball motion, from just about any angle but without any or only slight wrist-turn.

The variety of curves a batter must contend with is doubled by those coming from lefthanded pitchers and is quadrupled by "change-ups," with which both right- and lefthanded pitchers "take something off," or reduce the expected velocity, of their pitches.

The change-up, however gross or subtle, is essential to keep batters from timing their swings precisely. They may be anticipating a fastball or a curve—but how fast or how slow? Often slight variations in speed are undetectable even to the batters fooled by them, which is why they are fooled by them. Sometimes they are sensationally obvious to everybody in the park.

The slip, palm, and other blooper pitches we will look at in their own categories. More often they are slight variations in standard pitches that a pitcher must make to survive.

When he decided to throw change-ups late in the 1983 season, Frank Pastore of the Cincinnati Reds delivered a knockout blow to the St. Louis Cardinals' pennant chances. In a Sunday game in Cincinnati, the Cards had mauled him for seven hits and four runs in three innings. The next Friday, September 2, in St. Louis, the Cards looked forward to another base-hit feast off his consistent stuff, but Pastore shut them out on only four hits, striking out five, with deceptive off-speed pitching.

Three of his strikeouts came when he dared to throw slow stuff in fastball situations, with three-ball, two-strike counts. "You can fool good hitters with stuff like that," said his catcher, Allen Knicely. "We gave David Green five fastballs in a row to get three-two on him. Then we threw a change down the middle for a called third strike."

"It was a sweet taste," said Pastore, who had given up 165 hits in his previous 142 innings. "I decided it was time to change-up on my pitches."

If the fastball is God-given, the curve is coach-given. It is taught and can be learned. While the principles of curve pitching are universal because they are based upon the aerodynamic inevitabilities known as the Bernoulli and Wagner Effects, there is considerable variation in the teaching and learning of the mechanics of throwing them. In the shelves of how-to-pitch books you can find in most libraries, you will find contradictions in the best grips and deliveries for the same kinds of pitches—fingers with the seams or across them, for example. The best coaches insist upon the basic mechanics that they have found work best for most pitchers, but they also help pitchers adjust them to their physical and psychological peculiarities.

While the purpose of curve pitching is to keep batters from swinging to the right point at an exact instant, it is also a bedevilment to the pitchers. The pitcher cannot know precisely how the curve he is going to throw will behave. His confidence is eroded by the realization that he must make it behave within a reduced strike zone. Jim Konstanty, a pioneer relief specialist in the 1940s and 1950s with the Phillies and Yankees, put it this way: "If you pitch a curve high, it is murdered. If you throw it low, chances are it will break too low. As a consequence your real strike zone is reduced to about two feet, and that calls for real control." As arms tire in later innings, the curve becomes more uncertain, and pitchers tend to use it mainly to set batters up for more dependable key strikes with fastballs, sliders, or their "something else."

Sometimes, during warm-ups, a pitcher's curve will move like a killer shark, but when he calls on it in the first inning it floats plateward like a dead mackerel. But—and this is true of many no-hit games achieved with a perfect mixture of fastballs and curves—sometimes, after a discouraging warm-up, he goes to the mound and discovers his curve hooking in front of the batters and his fastball zipping past them. Thrown with renewed confidence, they hook and zip even better as he mows the batters down.

One reason often disregarded by his expectant fans (and sometimes by his managers and coaches) that a pitcher can "have good stuff out there" one game and "not a thing" the next, is that he is not a machine. Does he have a touch of flu that he is not going to let make him miss his turn? Is it something he ate? Was the ice bad in the seven highballs he drank last night? Is his wife home alone a thousand miles away with a sick child? Is he still rankled by the three errors the infield made that caused him to be charged with a loss on the three-hitter he pitched his last time out?

I think variations in a pitcher's effectiveness are due more frequently to changes in atmospheric pressure than most players, coaches, and fans realize. When the late Johnny Keane was managing the St. Louis Cardinals in the 1960s, I made some correlations between pitchers and their pitches and barometric readings from the weather bureau. I reviewed them with Johnny for an hour one afternoon. I showed him how Sam (Toothpick) Jones, throwing seeds, had beaten Juan Marichal of the Giants, whose curves were bending but not breaking, on a night of 29.6 inches of mercury. And how, a few nights later, Bob Gibson overcame two homers off fastballs in the early innings to set them down the rest of the way with curves and sliders on a night of 30.3. And so on. Johnny shook his head with gentle patience. "Maybe so," he said, "but air pressure, like rain or cold or heat, is the same for everybody out there. They see, and we see, what's working and what ain't, whether it's air pressure or a million other things, and adjust as we go. That's what makes us tick."

Maybe so. But if I were a betting man, I would add air pressure to other considerations before taking or giving the published odds on a game—though sometimes, as in the game described earlier that Bruce Sutter was pitching in St. Louis, the air pressure changes so rapidly that there wouldn't be time to get a bookie on the phone.

One of a pitcher's most difficult problems is to decide before every pitch, in agreement with his catcher, which of his pitches to throw and where to try to throw it. The batter must not know, and the catcher *must* know, what he is going to come in with.

The most disastrously unexpected pitch—a strike—in the history of the game was thrown by Hugh Casey in the 1941 World Series between the Brooklyn Dodgers and the New York Yankees. The Dodgers were down two games to one, but they were ahead in the ninth inning of the fourth game, 4–3, with two out and nobody on base— one out to go to tie the series. Old Hugh got two strikes on Tommy Henrich. Mickey Owen, the Dodger catcher, signaled for and expected a high, hard waste pitch. But Casey came in with a gorgeous spitter that sunk at the plate. Henrich swung and missed. Seeing it, the players and crowd believed the Dodgers had won, and swarmed onto the field. But Owen, lunging for the breaking ball, couldn't get a mitt on it. It took Henrich a moment to start for first as Owen chased after the ball, both of them dodging between players, cops, and fans. Henrich was safe at first. The Yanks then racked up a single and two doubles off Casey, won the game 7–4, and went on to win the world championship in the fifth game.

The catcher usually signals for the pitch, basing his suggestion on the count, the game situation, the batter's habits and weaknesses, what's working best for the pitcher, and so on. One finger down or against his leg is the fastball. Two fingers is Number Two—the Deuce—the curveball. Three for the slider, and four for a pitcher's "something else." Some pitchers have a greater variety. Murry Dickson had so many pitches that Joe Garagiola considered catching him barefooted so he could use his toes, too. Sometimes a fist, or a wave of the mitt, or touching the mask supplements or replaces the finger signal.

Though the signal may be an order from the bench, the pitcher customarily has the final say on what to throw. There are dozens of ways to shake off the catcher's sign without shaking the head. A twitch of the pitcher's glove may mean he agrees, or it may mean he is adding one to the signal for a fastball and is going to throw a curve. A touch of the bill of his cap may mean the pitcher is subtracting one from the Deuce and is coming in with Number One. Sometimes, after agreement, the pitcher looks in and shakes off two or three meaningless signs just to give the batter more to guess about—or to confuse a watchful base runner at second, or an off-duty pitcher watching through binoculars from an opening in the centerfield scoreboard.

Although stealing and reading signs and signals is as old as the game, it is not the most productive way to determine what a pitcher is going to throw in order to signal the batter what to expect. Opposing players and coaches may be able to see and count the catcher's fingers as well as the pitcher, but which flash is the one that signals the pitch? Besides, signals can be changed during a game, or even between pitches. The best way to determine what a pitcher is going to throw is to observe his habits and mannerisms—and those of other players and coaches—and identify unconsciously made telltale indications. Because knowing what pitch to expect swings the advantage to the batter, reading telltales is one of the high arts of baseball and one beyond the ken of fans.

The professional eyes of players, coaches, scouts, and front office people watch every pitcher's every move before and while he is getting set to throw every pitch. Does he handle or grip the ball discernibly different for the curve and the fastball or his "something else"? How about his set position, his kick? His other habits and rituals? What is he unknowingly telling us? Any such giveaways spotted are discussed at team meetings. Although kept as tight secrets, before long they usually get around the league as traded players shift allegiances.

On some clubs there are two or three coaches and players—a canny pinch hitter on the bench, an off-duty pitcher—who watch for, read, and relay telltales to the batter. "Let 'er rip!" shouted from bench to batter may tell him that a fastball is coming. A rapid clap of the hands from the third-base coach tells the batter to wait on the knuckler that's coming next.

After his fastball lost a couple of feet per second in velocity for the Yankees, Bob Turley became one of the best readers in the game. Bob found that Early Wynn, who pitched twenty-three years in the majors and won the Cy Young Award as the outstanding pitcher of

1959, was easy for a batter to read. "Early's nose served as the guidepost," Bob said after Early's retirement in 1963. "During the windup when he raised his hands high enough for the glove to blot out his nose, it meant a curve was coming. When the glove just reached the tip of his nose, a slider. When the glove came up not quite to the nose, a fastball. When he was going to throw a knuckler, his glove and hand reached no higher than chest level."

The Yankees batters used these readings to delay Wynn's 300th win in 1962, when Early's fastball had lost some zip. "Our batters waited for his glove to come up to just below his nose. That meant fastball and fastball almost invariably meant base hit," Turley recalled. Early won his 300th against the Kansas City Athletics, who were not reading him.

After both were safely in the Hall of Fame in the 1970s, Cool Papa Bell, who played all his years of great baseball in the Negro National League, enjoyed telling how he read a man-on-first habit of Bob Lemon of Cleveland, whom he had never before batted or run against, to score all the way from first without a play being made on him.

It happened on October 24, 1948, in an all-star exhibition game in Los Angeles. Cool Papa, then forty-five, was recruited to play in the game by his old buddy Satchel Paige, who at forty-three had just completed his rookie year in the majors. Satch organized the visiting team and Bob Feller, his pitching teammate on the Indians, organized the home team. Cool Papa doubled off Bob his first time up. Next time, batting eighth ahead of Satch, he singled. Now Satch was going to sacrifice-bunt him to second. Cool Papa had seen Bob pitch several games from the rightfield pavilion at Sportsman's Park in St. Louis, the designated roost of black fans.

"It was second nature for me," said the old base thief, "to study all pitchers for what I could learn to get a jump. I saw that Lemon, once he looked hard at a runner on first, didn't look again. So he looked and looked away, and I was gone."

Satch dropped a perfect bunt to the left in no-man's land. Roy Partee, the catcher (Red Sox and Browns), scrambled out to the ball ahead of Lemon and the charging third baseman. By this time Cool Papa was into second. Seeing third base untended, he wheeled for third. Partee sprinted for third, past his errant third baseman. Cool Papa, there ahead of him, now saw that no one was covering home. He ran past the surprised Partee's waving tag and flew in to score.

Burleigh Grimes, who was one of seventeen major league pitchers given granddaddy rights to continue to throw the spitball after it and other doctored pitches were declared illegal beginning in 1920, had good success throwing his spitter for the Brooklyn Dodgers against every team but the Philadelphia Phillies. They were taking his spitter and jumping on his fastball. New signs and changing signs between pitches did not deter the mystifying onslaught. From a traded player, Burleigh learned that it was because his cap was too tight. When he faked moistening the ball but was going to throw his good fastball, the peak of his cap did not move. But when he was going to wet it, his jaws worked to produce good slippery elm saliva, and the peak of his cap bobbled. Burleigh got a looser cap and had no more trouble with the Phillies reading his pitches.

Only long after his retirement did Burleigh learn of another telltale that tipped off the Cleveland Indians to the spitters he was throwing while pitching for the Brooklyn Dodgers in the World Series of 1920. But it was not his own unconscious giveaway that enabled the Indians to knock him out of the box in the fourth inning of the fifth game. Years later, Jack McCallister, a coach for the Indians, told him how they had picked up a telltale indication from Pete Kilduff, the Dodger second baseman. When he saw that Burleigh had the signal for a spitter, Pete would toss a handful of dust into his glove to give him a better grip on the slippery surface of the ball if it was hit to him. Dust in his glove meant spitter to the batter and defeat for Burleigh.

It may be coincidence that Deuce is the nickname for both the curveball and the devil. My father did not think so. As he saw my Irish interest in the dissembling curves conflict with my Norwegian concern for the morality of their use, he said it stood to reason that God could not enjoy the game He loved the best if He took a hand in favoring one team or player over another. Dad said that God permitted the trickery of the curve and its crooked cousins, as He did the wiles of Satan, to give man free will and to put the outcome of interesting confrontations in doubt. Will Eve eat the apple or won't she? And what happens next?

"But I'll tell you this, son, there are some great curve pitchers that never doctored a ball in their lives. Maybe," he concluded, "they thought it was wrong—or maybe they didn't have to."

Such a one, a tricky pitcher of honest curves, was Warren Spahn, whose gentlemanly dignity defied all efforts to stick a nickname on him. I went out to see him pitch against the Cardinals every chance I got during the more than two decades when he pitched for the Braves of Boston and Milwaukee. I used to find myself secretly hoping he would pitch out of jams, and silently applauding his craft when he did. I would check the box scores of every game he pitched. Though I reached middle age as he continued to pitch during the 1960s, I had as severe a case of hero worship as any kid. His major league records—most games won (363) and most seasons (13) with twenty or more wins by a lefthanded pitcher, seven consecutive years leading the league in complete games, seventeen consecutive years with 100 or more strikeouts—seemed to become my records.

Early in his career, when his fastball still jumped and he mixed it with two curves, a wide hook that seemed to come in from first base and a darter that seemed to break on the plate, I merely marveled. Later, when he began to throw a screwball, down and away from righthanded batters and low and in to lefthanders, and extremely effective against both, I felt that I was out on the mound standing in his spikes.

Though he was blessed with a powerful physique—six feet tall and 185 supple and gracefully coordinated pounds—he seemed to me to be the epitome of the crafty curveball pitcher of my fantasies. I was surprised and only slightly disillusioned to learn that he was a pitching fundamentalist, who did not believe in—or teach—the need for a variety of tricky pitches. During spring training in 1971, when he was a pitching instructor for the Cardinals at their new training complex in St. Petersburg, I interviewed him during a relaxing cloudburst. Not knowing how long the rain would last, but knowing he was working with twenty young pitchers, I went right for the jugular.

"The main thing—the main thing about fooling the batters the way you did for so many years—what is it?"

"Comfort," he said. "Be comfortable on the rubber so you can get maximum leverage on your pitches without putting too much strain on your arm."

"Besides comfort?"

"Control. That was the hardest thing for me to learn starting out."

"And?"

"Concentrate—concentrate on a fastball, curve, and change-up. If you've got control of those three, you've got the essentials."

"The three C's of pitching. . . ."

"And one DC—don't copy anybody else. It's you throwing out there, not somebody else."

"But your trick pitches," I persisted. "Your screwball. . . ."

He nodded his dismissal of them. "The slider, screwball, knuckler. . . . They're fine pitches for older arms, but—you asked about fooling batters? You've got to learn how to pitch to different kinds of batters. When I see a batter with his back knee bent, I figure him for a low-ball hitter and keep the ball up on him. If he's hitting off his front foot, he's a high-ball hitter. Some great hitters, like Musial, hit low and high pitches equally well. . . ." The rain was easing off, and he got up to go to work. "One thing, though, to keep a batter guessing, you've got to throw to his strengths as well as his weaknesses. But—" as he waved goodbye, "you'd better have more than three fingers on the ball when you do it."

My favorite story told by another hero, Stan Musial (in the book he wrote with Bob Broeg, *The Man's Own Story*, Doubleday, 1964), is about Warren Spahn. "He's the only pitcher ever to walk a batter to face me," Stan relates. "Back in 1957 when the Cardinals were threatening Milwaukee's league lead, Fred Haney brought Spahn in from the bullpen in the ninth inning to protect a one-run lead. He walked the batter in front of me to set up an inning-ending double play. I obliged."

In Warren Spahn I saw the great curveball pitcher that I had no way or chance of becoming. It has occurred to me since that I chose as my hero one that both my father and mother could have admired without reservations.

Among the many reasons that Donald (Big D) Drysdale became the other great pitching hero of my middle age was that by never missing a turn he contributed more to the success of his team than just the victories he won on the mound. Only Walter Johnson and Warren Spahn were in his class in this respect. Year in and year out, from 1956 when he joined the Dodgers in Brooklyn until 1969 when he wound up his career with them in Los Angeles, he took his turn. Often he would miss a day of rest, in the pressure of a pennant race, to take the place of an ailing starter, including his Hall of Fame teammate, Sandy Koufax. Moreover, he was ready to come out and pitch late-inning relief when needed. For nine years in a row, after moving to Los Angeles in 1958, he pitched in forty or more games. And with a good fastball and a complete assortment of curves, including a sharp slider, he pitched brilliantly and with tight control. In a total of 518 games for the Dodgers, he pitched 3,432 innings (including the major league record of 58 consecutive scoreless innings), won 209 games (including six consecutive shutouts, another major league record), and struck out 2,486 batters with only 855 bases on balls. If the records could show how much his ability and willingness to take his turn without fail helped the other pitchers, his manager, and his team, he would have made the Hall of Fame long before his selection in 1984.

Joe DiMaggio in 1939, when he led the American League with a .381 batting average and hit 30 homers. Even in retirement Joe wouldn't quite admit that Johnny Allen's sliders had been doctored; though come to think of it, he added, "I did not in those days miss sliders by a foot." *The Sporting News*

Johnny Vander Meer of the Cincinnati Reds, only man ever to pitch consecutive no-hit, no-run games. *The Sporting News*

CHAPTER EIGHT

The Screwball
(Alias Fadeaway)

The first screwball I saw in flight was thrown one summer in the late twenties, when I was bat boy for the Lake Park, Minnesota, Beavers. One of my privileges was to catch warm-ups in the bullpen, whose personnel that day consisted of a long-armed, pot-bellied fifty-year-old itinerant ringer named Teddy Swanson, and myself. We had paid his train fare from Pelican Rapids and offered him a share of our winnings, if any, to relieve if needed in our winner-take-all game with the Audubon Barn Burners. A full share would fetch $10–$12.

As he loosened up, throwing to me, he told me he had left his fastball at home, so his Number One was a nickel curve, Number Two an out, Number Three a drop, and Number Four a knuckler. When he was ready, I signaled for each in turn, several times in a row. "One more," he said after I had plowed the dirt with my chin while smothering Number Four. It soared in and took a sudden inward drop that I missed by a foot, and that would have hit a right-handed batter on his back foot.

"That Number Five of yours is the first indrop I ever saw a righthander throw."

"That pitch you missed is a fadeaway," he said, showing me how he gripped it on the top seams, with greatest pressure on the second finger, and released it with his wrist turning counterclockwise all the way from inside to outside, causing the ball to spin clockwise. "I learned it from a fella who learned it from Christy Mathewson his ownself."

Of course I knew about Christy's famous fadeaway, but, already convinced that a pitched ball could be made to perform as many tricks as a poodle, I had envisioned it as a ball that seemed to dissolve in the air as it neared the plate. By the time I could make it bend a little myself, I knew it as the screwball. (I first heard the "scroogie" endearment for it in the sixties.)

Although Christopher (Big Six) Mathewson made the pitch luminous as his fadeaway, he would have been famous without it. He had everything else, too: fastball and curve (out, outdrop, and drop), and a change-up on all of them, and control. Along with Ol' Pete Alexander and Satchel Paige, he ranks with the supreme control artists of the game. I call up the memory of Christy here because he is identified with the screwball—just as Ol' Pete and Satchel, who also had everything, are identified, respectively, with deadly control and the "hesitation" pitch, which is why I will discuss them later as specialists.

When in 1900 the New York Giants brought Christy up from Norfolk in the Virginia League, he was big—6'1" and 195 pounds—with a strong arm and a roundhouse curve, which, he recalled when his pitching days were over, "was no more than a big, slow outdrop that I had been fooling batters with in the minor leagues." George Davis, manager of the Giants, told him it would be of no use to him in the major leagues, and it wasn't. After pitching and losing three games in which he gave up 20 bases on balls and 32 runs, he found himself back down in Norfolk. Determined to come back with what it took to win in the National League, he learned to throw a "drop ball" and practiced throwing strikes "away from the center of the plate."

The Giants lost possession of Mathewson to the Cincinnati Redlegs in the draft, but Davis coveted him and finagled to trade Amos Rusie, then at trail's end, to get the rookie back. This trade, offering much for little, was a dumb one for the Redlegs but not for Buck Ewing, their manager, who was expecting to join the Giant organization, which he soon did. Thus, in 1901, Mathewson began his sixteen-year career with the Giants.

Though he won 20 games, losing 17, with 215 strikeouts and only 92 bases on balls that year, Christy's rise toward baseball immortality was assured in July, 1902, when John Joseph (Little Napoleon) McGraw began his thirty-year career as manager of the Giants, during which the Giants won ten National League pennants and three world championships. (In the ten World Series games Mathewson pitched for McGraw, his earned-run average was 1.15.) McGraw came to New York from Baltimore, where, as manager and scrappy infielder, he had earned a reputation (preceding that of Ty Cobb's) as the most determined and relentless edge-finder and creator in every aspect of the game, including the temperature of the baseballs.

Christy recalled, for example, how McGraw looked into the possibility that amputation of a pitcher's finger would enable him to pitch as marvelous a curve as that of Three-Fingered Brown of the Chicago Cubs. Mordecai Brown, born in 1876, was given Centennial as a middle name as part of his family's celebration of the one-hundredth birthday of the United States of America, but his nickname came from losing the forefinger on his right hand to a feed cutter as an Indiana farm boy. Compensating for its loss by increasing the pressure of his second finger on the seam, Three-Fingered Brown threw a mean curve, which was his best pitch in winning 208 games and losing 111 during an eleven-year National League career.

McGraw ordered his pitchers, in practice, to throw their curves without pressure from their forefingers while he judged the effects. He shook his head and said he guessed that it didn't give them new and better curves. "It's lucky for you fellows that it doesn't," he told his troops, "because if I thought it did, I'd have a surgeon out here tomorrow."

It was when he began pitching for McGraw that Mathewson began throwing his fadeaway. Though McGraw could not use Rube Foster, the control artist of early black baseball, on the mound, there was no restriction against using him as a teacher of privileged white rookies. Rube worked with young Christy on his control and, some say, taught him his fadeaway.

"It is a slow curve pitched with the motion of a fastball, but it breaks toward a righthanded batter," Christy said of the pitch. From that description, one would think it was sort of a slider screwball, thrown without much reverse wrist-turn; but Christy must have turned his wrist more than he realized. "Many people have asked me why I do not use my fadeaway more often when it is so effective," he went on. "It is a very hard pitch to deliver. Pitching it ten or twelve times a game kills my arm, so I save it for the pinches."

And that is the reason why the screwball is the least popular of the curves as a main pitch. A great many pitchers have mastered it and used it "in the pinches," as Christy did, but only one, King Carl Hubbell, had the arm to throw it as his bread-and-butter pitch—in the way that Walter Johnson did his fastball—over the course of a long and great career.

With his fadeaway and with his control of everything he pitched, Christy Mathewson, the Big Six, became a baseball immortal. No one since 1900 in the National League has pitched as many consecutive innings (68) without a base on balls. With Ol' Pete Alexander he holds the National League record for most games won (373). He pitched shutouts in the first, third, and fifth games of the World Series of 1905 against Connie Mack's Philadelphia Athletics. Twenty years after his retirement and eleven years after his death in 1925, Mathewson was voted into the Hall of Fame in the first election.

Carl Owen Hubbell, born in Carthage, Missouri, was only two years old when Mathewson won the 1905 World Series for the Giants. The future king of the screwball became a Giant himself in 1928, when McGraw was still calling the shots and everything else. When he began his professional career in the Oklahoma State League, Hubbell, a tall and wiry young man of twenty, had no ball of fire or much of anything else, including control. It was not until 1925, pitching for Oklahoma City in the Western League, that he showed major league potential with a 17 and 13 won-lost record even without decent control, as indicated by the 108 bases on balls he gave up while striking out 102 batters. The Detroit Tigers signed him for a looksee in spring training, but did not like what they saw and released him to Beaumont in the Texas League, where Giant scouts liked what *they* did see in 1928, especially his 116 strikeouts against only 45 bases on balls, mainly with the screwball. Hubbell finished the 1928 season with the Giants, winning 10 games for them while giving up only 21 bases on balls in the 124 innings he pitched. McGraw knew he had another fadeaway winner.

Unlike other screwball pitchers, King Carl did not throw it as a diversion from his other pitches; he threw his other pitches as a diversion from it. The uncounted thousands of times he turned his wrist throwing it actually twisted his wrist outside-in permanently. His turned-in left arm became the King's identifying scepter. Perhaps it was this acquired deformity that enabled him to throw the screwball effortlessly in the 3,591 innings he pitched in his sixteen years with the Giants; since his wrist was already turned he could bring it down in a fastball motion with a built-in drop curve.

Thrown lefthanded, his screwball broke in and down to lefthanded batters, out and down to righthanders. Its effectiveness against both was demonstrated spectacularly in the 1934 All-Star game when it seemed to have a life of its own, like a puppet, as it struck out five Hall of Fame batters in a row. The first two, Babe Ruth and Lou Gehrig, were lefthanders; the next three, Jimmie Foxx, Al Simmons, and Joe Cronin, were righthanders. It did not matter; the screwball got them.

On July 2, 1933, as an example of the apparently effortless control he had of it, Hubbell pitched an 18-inning 1–0 victory over the St. Louis Cardinals without surrendering a base on balls. One of the 253 games he won for the Giants was a no-hitter against the Pittsburgh Pirates on May 8, 1929. King Carl was voted into the Hall of Fame as soon as he became eligible in 1947.

Many pitchers have thrown the screwball effectively, and a few others—including Cy Blanton of the Pirates, Tug McGraw of the New York Mets and Philadelphia Phillies, and Tom Brewer of the Boston Red Sox—have depended mainly upon it. Its most recent successful practitioner is Fernando Valenzuela of the Los Angeles Dodgers, who used it as he won eight games in a row to begin the strike-shortened season of 1981, before he was twenty-one years old.

When Hubbell saw him pitch, he said the young Mexican, also a lefthander, was throwing the best screwball he had seen in forty years of his retirement, because it came out of an over-the-top motion, like his fastball, and broke sharply down at the plate. Valenzuela is still thousands of innings away from proving his durability as a major league screwball pitcher, but he seems to be off to a good start.

98

Tommy Byrne of
the New York
Yankees, inventor
of the "kimono
ball," and, *inset*,
the grip he used
to throw his fork-
ball. *The Sporting
News*

The "Old Perfes-
ser," Casey Sten-
gel, at the height
of his reign as
skipper of the
Yankees, in
1955. Casey fa-
vored legalizing
the spitball: "Let
them revive the
spitter and help
the pitchers make
a living," he de-
clared. *The
Sporting News*

Harry (The Cat) Brecheen won three games for the St. Louis Cardinals against the Boston Red Sox in the 1946 World Series. *The Sporting News*

The assortment of pitches thrown by Murry Dickson was so varied that his catcher, Joe Garagiola, considered using his toes as well as fingers to signal for pitches. *The Sporting News*

Harvey Haddix
pitched a perfect
game for twelve
innings against
the Milwaukee
Braves for the
Pittsburgh Pi-
rates, only to lose
in the thirteenth.
*The Sporting
News*

CHAPTER NINE

The Slider (Alias Nickel Curve)

"A slider is either a fastball with a very small slow break or a curveball with a very small fast break," Chuck Dressen said about it when managing the Milwaukee Braves.

Though its heritage goes back, like almost everything else in baseball, to the formative years of the game, it suddenly became an addition in the arsenal of many pitchers, especially those with good fastballs, in the early 1950s. While there are almost as many versions of its origins as there are spinners of baseballs and baseball yarns, there is general, though not unanimous, agreement about what it is, and even on how it is thrown.

The consensus is that it is, as the Dressen definition indicates, a high-velocity pitch thrown with fastball motion, which comes in like a fastball until, near the plate, it takes a quick veer, or curve. Like the fastball, it is thrown with little or no wrist-turn. Unlike the release of the fastball, the top fingers along the seams pull down and sideways, giving the ball lateral spin. The firm wrist does not diminish velocity as much as the wrist-turn of the regular curve will do, but the side pressure of the fingers does, ideally, make it a split second slower than an up-spinning fastball. Its delivery and spin are frequently likened to the delivery and spiral of a forward pass in football, which cannot be thrown with wrist-turn.

Like the other pitches in baseball, and almost everything else in life, there are good sliders and bad ones. The good slider is thrown, and looks to the batter, like the pitcher's fastball, but it comes in just a little slower and takes a sharp break of only a few inches. A bad slider, usually the result of unconscious wrist-turn, has too little velocity and a more gentle curve.

"I think a slider is really rough," said Elston Howard, the New York Yankee catcher, when it was coming into style, "if," he added, "it's working that day." Clyde McCullough, catching for the Chicago Cubs then, agreed that, well thrown, "it's a hell of a pitch. But I have seen more home runs hit off sliders than any other pitch." Clay Hopper, managing Montreal in the International League, defined the slider as "a curveball that's just been hit for three bases."

But the good slider, as a variation of speed and break between the fastball and a regular curve, is in the opinion of the best hitters as tough a pitch to hit safely as comes down the pike. Ted Williams said so. Stan Musial appreciated the extra split second it gave him to pull the trigger, but added: "You can't go up there with a forty-ounce bat and expect to change the snap of your wrist to meet a breaking pitch that's coming up looking like a fastball."

I used to hear pitchers call it, or something very like it, a "fast curve" before it was generally called, more often in contempt than respect, the nickel curve. I fooled around with it, as I did with every pitch I saw or heard about, but did not have the finger strength or knack to make anything but a lollipop out of it, even in town ball.

A case can be made for Elmer Stricklett, the old Brooklyn spitballer, as the man who brought it to the major leagues. Ed Walsh, who used it well in the latter years of his Hall of Fame career with the White Sox, said that Elmer taught him the pitch in 1904. But in 1953, when it was becoming popular, Bucky Walters, mound coach of the Milwaukee Braves, said he learned the pitch from Charles (Chief) Bender of the Philadelphia Athletics, who had used it in the 4–0 no-hitter the Chief pitched against the Cleveland Indians on May 12,

1910. "I never said it was a slider, though," Bucky said, "because Bender didn't have a name for it."

Frank Shellenback, the renowned spitballer who was condemned to pitching in the minors because the Chicago White Sox did not list him as an established major league spitball pitcher for the 1920 season, also threw the slider before it was known as such. As the New York Giants' pitching coach, Frank was credited by both Sal Maglie and Larry Jansen with teaching them to throw the slider as he had thrown it for years.

One reason why the pitch came into vogue was the expansion of the major leagues and the dilution of pitching talent beginning in 1961. To be effective major league pitchers, the minor league pitchers brought up to fill in major league rosters usually needed "something else." As Mel Harder, then pitching coach for the Cleveland Indians, put it: "A fellow with only a fair fastball and curve needs another pitch, and he can usually master the slider." The good pitchers, too, especially those with great fastballs, added it to their mix, and almost every great pitcher of the last thirty years has employed it to increase the odds against a batter's guessing correctly what the next pitch will be. Old-timers like Frankie Frisch and Rogers Hornsby grumbled that it was nothing but the nickel curve of their time, but others hailed it as "the pitch that changed baseball" and that made .285 hitters out of .300 hitters.

One of the best to make use of it was Bob Lemon of the Cleveland Indians. As versatile as Tony Mullane and Jim White, he came up through the minors to Cleveland as an infielder-outfielder whose poor control kept him from being a dependable fastball pitcher. He played as a utility infielder, both at third base and shortstop, in 1941–42, and then after three years of military service came back in 1946–47 as a pitcher-outfielder. For the remaining eleven years of his playing career, however, he pitched (and hit seven home runs in 108 at-bats as a pitcher in 1949). He could control the wicked slider he developed better than he could his curve, and he used it with his fastball to win 207 games for Cleveland and earn election to the Hall of Fame in 1976.

But the supreme slider specialist is Steve Carlton. Since coming up with the St. Louis Cardinals, Carlton has been pitching major league baseball for nearly twenty years, the last twelve for the Philadelphia Phillies. During those years he has struck out more batters than any pitcher who has ever lived or is ever likely to live. Few who know him doubt that, barring accidental injury or onslaught of disease, Carlton will be striking out batters long after Nolan Ryan, his rival in total strikeouts, has called it quits. At forty, Steve tells his intimates—the only persons to whom he tells anything, other than the time of day—that he expects to continue pitching into the nineties—the century's, not his.

While his slider is his best pitch—his fastball rarely exceeds 90 MPH and his good curve is mainly a diversion—those who know him best attribute his amazing career to his unusually superb physique, which he maintains and improves with daily and secret exercises, and his intense obsession with throwing unhittable strikes. The slider, which is a physically demanding pitch, happens to be the instrument of his body and will.

Tim McCarver, who caught him for both the Cardinals and the Phillies, tells how Steve stretches on the training table and closes his eyes before going out to the mound. "He is thinking outer lane and inner lane," McCarver said. "He doesn't think about anything over the middle of the plate. He never thinks about a batter being a low-ball hitter or anything like that. To him the batter is just an impediment. He's just out there to pitch past him to the catcher."

Claude Osteen, the Phillies' pitching coach, insists Carlton is not thinking strikeouts: "The first thing with Lefty is winning. Win. Win. Win." As is the way of the baseball world, Carlton has lost games that were his best strikeout performances. For St. Louis in 1969, he once struck out nineteen New York Mets and lost 4–3 on two homers by Ron Swoboda. Two years later, pitching for the Phillies, he struck out fifteen Mets and lost on the first home run hit by John Stearns in 736 at-bats.

Whatever else Steve Carlton achieves with his slider in the years left to him, he is on his way into the Hall of Fame, with more money earned and with less to say about how he did it than any other pitcher.

With two outs in the ninth inning, the Yankees' Yogi Berra misses Ted Williams's high foul ball to prolong Allie Reynolds's second no-hitter of the 1951 season. Reynolds is at left, and the umpire is Cal Hubbard. Williams fouled the next pitch, and Berra caught it for the third out. *The Sporting News*

Cool Papa Bell, at the age of forty-five, stole second, third, and home off Bob Lemon in exhibition play. It was Bell who tipped off the Cleveland Indians that the ageing Satchel Paige was the strike-throwing relief pitcher they wanted. This photo was made in 1930. *The Sporting News*

Leroy (Satchel) Paige in 1948, when at the age of forty-three he finally made it to the majors with the Cleveland Indians. Bob Feller is seated with him. *Associated Press*

CHAPTER TEN

The Knuckleball
(Alias Mariposa)

The hardest thing to say about the knuckleball is anything true. It isn't even a knuckleball, except the way that old Jess Haines threw it. It is a fingertip ball, except when thrown as a fingernail ball. It is thrown off, or pushed off, the tips or nails of two fingers, except when it is thrown off one, or three fingers. It is a slow, tantalizing pitch that is sometimes thrown with greater velocity than other curves. It is the most difficult pitch to hit safely or far, but no pitcher who relied mainly on it has ever been elected to Baseball's Hall of Fame.

Many fans, including this one, and many knowledgeable observers and historians of the game, believe that Hoyt Wilhelm's mastery of the knuckleball, with which he bewildered batters until he was nearly fifty years old, should have secured him a place at Cooperstown. We can only hope that ultimately the undeniable facts of his record will dispel the clouds of doubt about his worthiness that seem to exist in the minds of so many of the voting populace of sports writers. Why they think he does not belong there may give them more challenging essays to write than the recitals of his accomplishments, about which more later.

In all the years—though nobody knows just how many—the knuckleball has been deceiving batters, it has been called as many things as it has ways to get to the plate, or wherever else it may go. It's the knuckler, the flutterball, the crazy butterfly (the mariposa magicrosa of our Hispanic players), the fingertip pitch, the tantalizer, the dancer, the butterfly (mariposa bianca), and "that thing."

It is one of the easiest pitches to learn to throw and is so much fun to throw that it may well be the most frequently thrown pitch in base-ball—not in games, but along the sidelines during warm-ups, and not by pitchers but by infielders and outfielders enjoying its idiosyncracies and perhaps dreaming, as Mickey Mantle did, of mastering it "and adding ten years to my career."

Pepper Martin once had his dream come true of pitching it in a game. As Frankie Frisch told it: "He was always monkeying around with a knuckler, and he could really throw it. One time I had a bunch of sore-arm pitchers on the Cards and we got a doubleheader going. My first thrower gets his lumps and they have the bases full and no-body out, so I say to myself, 'Hell, here's a chance to get that Martin off my back about pitching.' So I send him in, and he gets one guy on a fly, and the next guy hits into a double play. He gets the first hitter in the next inning and then he calls me over and says: 'Get another pitcher. I can't raise my arm.' After that, I have no more trouble with Pepper wanting to pitch."

It is, as accurately as you can say anything about it, a spinless or nearly spinless pitch, launched like a fastball with little or no wrist-turn but usually with a limber wrist. The knuckles on the guiding fingers, usually two, are withdrawn from the ball like coiled springs. As the ball zips away from the fingertips, the thumb and other fingers are opened to take the friction of their grip off the surface.

As the ball sails out, spinless, the vagaries of its flight are governed by the flow of air on the irregularities of its tilting seams, and by grav-ity. But it does not always curve or break downward. Sometimes as it nears the plate the seams tilt, like the airfoil of an ascending airplane, to make it defy gravity and fly up. It could, however, just as unpre-dictably take a comparable sudden swerve down or away or in.

The action of the knuckler, however, is much greater against the wind than with it, and in high pressure than in low. Thrown with a stiff wind behind it into sultry air, a knuckler has little going for it except the pitcher's reputation.

There are several other compelling reasons why it is not a reliable instrument of deception for most pitchers. Knowing that it is going to be taking its own devilish time getting to the catcher, base runners steal on it. Even Ernie Lombardi, the great catcher and hitter for the Cincinnati Reds and the New York Giants in the thirties and forties (who some say might have been a .500 hitter if he could have beaten out his share of infield hits and made it safely to first on normal line singles through the infield) once tried to steal on one of Freddy Fitzsimmons's laziest knucklers in Ebbets Field; he was thrown out by only ten feet, according to Beans Reardon, the umpire who called the play and told me about it. Two other reasons for its lack of universal popularity are (a) while easy to throw, it is hard to control, and (b) its final sudden swerves often make it as uncatchable as it is unhittable. Bob Uecker, a clubhouse wit who caught for one of the best knucklers ever, used to say that the best way to catch Hoyt Wilhelm's mariposa was to use a 38-inch mitt, wait till the ball stopped rolling, and pick it up.

Rick Ferrell, who caught for the Washington Senators in the wartime forties when the starting rotation consisted of four knucklers (and who had 44 passed balls charged to him in one season), offered more statesmanlike advice to catchers. He advised a half-standing position instead of the usual crouch, enabling quicker lateral movement and a belly-flop on a ball in the dirt. "Relax and give with the pitch," he would tell them. "Don't fight it or challenge it." Mike Sandlock, another veteran catcher of the knuckler (then with the Pittsburgh Pirates), affirmed the teachings of Ferrell: "The knuckler's like a dame. If you reach for it, you're licked. You've got to wait until it reaches for you."

Walker Cooper, when catching for the St. Louis Cardinals, solved the knuckler problem by avoiding it. When Murry Dickson added it to his already amazing mix of pitches, Walker told him that if he needed it to stay up with the Cardinals he might as well pack his bag, "because I ain't gonna call it for you." And to Max Lanier, who also developed a wicked knuckler, Walker said: "If you can't win without that up here, you'd better get another mule and another acre of ground."

The reason so many pitchers tried their hand (or fingertips) at the knuckleball was to replace the spitter and other doctored balls that were outlawed in 1920. But the origin of the knuckler goes way back. Ed Summers of the Detroit Tigers, who used it unsuccessfully in two games against the Cubs in the World Series of 1908, said he learned it from an old-timer who threw it sidearm in the early eighties.

The most credible claimant for making the knuckler a fixture in the majors was Ed Rommel, who used it to become a star in Connie Mack's rotation for the Philadelphia Athletics. On the strength of the effectiveness of the spitter that he had been throwing in the minors at Newark, he was called up to the majors by Philadelphia for the 1920 season, but was told to take his illegal spitter and go home. A Baltimore plumber named Cutter Dreuery, a retired minor league pitcher, heard his sad story and taught him to throw the knuckleball. Ed threw it a few times, and Cutter told him, "You can control it better than I ever could." So Ed took it to the majors and won 27 games with it for the seventh-place Athletics in 1922. After retirement he became an umpire, and had to learn to call it, too.

Ted Lyons, of the Chicago White Sox, learned to throw the knuckler from a picture of Ed's grip. A big strong kid out of Baylor University, Ted took his God-given fastball directly to Chicago in 1923 and was, like Feller, an instant star, pitching a no-hitter against the Red Sox in 1926. When he developed a sore arm, he copied Eddie's grip. "It gave me a new lease on life," he said. It also helped him to last another twenty years with the White Sox, and won him entry, in 1955, into the Hall of Fame.

The knuckleball's spitter-like behavior, as he threw it, was why Freddy Fitzsimmons called it his "dry spitter" during the nineteen years (1925–43) he used it to win 217 games for the New York Giants and Brooklyn Dodgers. Fat Fred (who at 5'11" and 205 pounds might better have been nicknamed Muscles) made three different pitches out of its spinless deception, throwing it fast, medium, and oh so slow.

Another long-lived master of the knuckler, twenty years (1933–53) in both leagues, was Emil (Dutch) Leonard, who once complained about a call to umpire Cal Hubbard: "That pitch was over the plate on the way in." "No, Emil," Cal said, "that pitch was all over the park, and it was over the plate on the way back." Dutch gave the nine best years (1938–46) of his knuckleball to Clark Griffith's cellar-dwelling Washington Senators (for whom he won more games than any other pitcher except Walter Johnson), and in 1945 he was joined by three other knucklers—Johnny Niggeling, Roger Wolff, and Mickey Haefner—to form the only all-knuckleball rotation that major league base-ball has known. They came within one-and-a-half games of winning the war-tattered American League pennant. Between the four of them, they had three different ways of throwing their knucklers. Dutch and Mickey released it off two fingers, Roger off three, and Johnny (then forty-one) off only one. Such variations made it more difficult for bat-ters to get used to a steady diet of knucklers. How Rick Ferrell, their catcher, retained his sanity would make an interesting doctoral thesis on ways of coping with frustration.

The knuckler is what gave the heroic career of Johnny Lindell a dramatic ending. He came up to Marse Joe McCarthy of the Yankees in 1942 as a pitcher with a knuckler. So McCarthy made him his leftfielder. Well, the kid was big (6'4", 210), fast, and a fine hitter, but the compelling reason for the conversion was McCarthy's distrust of the knuckler. "When the ball breaks," he said of it, "the catcher misses it. If it doesn't break, the batter hits it out of sight."

After eight solid years with the Yankees—he batted .324 in the three World Series the Yankees played during his tenure—Johnny drifted down to the Hollywood Stars of the Pacific Coast League, and dusted off his old knuckler. In 1952 he won 24 games with it and the next year, at thirty-six, was back in the majors for a final season, first with the Pirates, then with the Phillies.

From Pops Haines to Schoolboy Rowe, it would take a full page just to list the pitchers whose major league careers were extended and enhanced by their use of the knuckler.

Because of the inherent unpredictability of their pitches—passed balls, wild pitches, stolen bases—the knuckleball specialists have mostly been starting pitchers, and are rarely called upon to save tight games in late innings. The few who have been relievers are those who can throw key strikes with it.

One who could was Wilbur Wood. As a nineteen-year-old, already looking like a roly-poly bear looking for a cave to sleep out the winter, he came up with the Boston Red Sox in 1961 as a knuckleball spe-cialist and pitched a few innings in relief with moderate success until he was traded to Pittsburgh, where he continued, because of his nearly two-to-one strikeout to bases on balls ratio, as a reliable spot reliever. Sent to the Chicago White Sox in 1967, he worked an average of about 120 innings a season through the 1970 season. At that point it dawned on the Sox that his effortless delivery made him a tireless workhorse. Until 1971, when he became a starting pitcher, he had started only 21 games in his previous ten years in the major leagues. During his last five years he started 224 games, relieved in only one, and achieved one of the most remarkable records in baseball history. Pitching for one of the most inept teams of that or almost any other time, his won-loss record was 22–13 in 1971, 24–17 in 1972, 24–20 in 1973, 20–19 in 1974, and 16–20 in 1975. While winning 164 games (22 of them shutouts) and losing 156 in his seventeen major league seasons, he pitched 2,684 innings, struck out 1,411 batters, and gave up only 724 bases on balls—with the knuckleball!

All of the great relief pitchers, whether versatile pitchers or specialists, were and are of necessity control artists, who could come into a game and throw hard-to-hit strikes, sometimes with the ball-strike count already against them. Of premium value while their ability lasts, they are legion. But changing conditions, and the increasing sophistication of the pitching talents put together to comprise modern pitching staffs, make it difficult to compare their merits and to separate the master relievers from good journeymen pitchers doing their jobs.

When starters get their lumps early, a manager now has a choice of left- or righthanded middle relievers to take over, sometimes to pitch to a single batter, more often to try to go as far as they can. Meanwhile the ace short reliever is there waiting, knowing he will not be called upon unless the game is in delicate balance with an inning or two to go.

A generation of pitchers ago, it was common practice to bring in one of the starting pitchers to pitch an inning or two of relief, put out the fire, and while he was at it get the loosening-up exercise he needed to be ready for his next start. The statistical definition of a "save"— holding a one- or two-run lead from the seventh inning on—gives "save" records only since 1969. The leader, with 272 through 1982, was Rollie Fingers, whose sore arm did not permit him to finish the season or to "save" the World Series for the Milwaukee Brewers from the St. Louis Cardinals. Second in saves since 1969, with 219, is Albert W. (Sparky) Lyle, who holds the major league record for most consecutive appearances as a reliever. Toiling for Boston, New York, Texas, and Chicago in the American League and Philadelphia in the National League, he pitched as a reliever in a total of 899 games from July 4, 1967, through the 1982 season with the Phillies and White Sox. Other leaders in "saves," Mike Marshall, Richard (Goose) Gossage, Bruce Sutter, Kent Tekulve, to name a few, are still embellishing their records in this category. The names of many other consistently dependable relievers—Johnny Murphy, Ace Adams, Ken Trinkle, Firpo Marberry—tend to fade like pickets in a fence in the long perspective of baseball history, their records diminishing in the blur of numbers in the record books, but remembered vividly by those who saw them come in to throw tough strikes when only tough strikes could save a game.

But both memories and the numbers he put in the books attest to the unique greatness of Hoyt Wilhelm as a reliever and, though briefly, as a starting pitcher. The only great knuckleball reliever and—taking into account the nonexistent and ambiguous statistical measurements of "saves," of which his record is a victim—Wilhelm was perhaps the greatest relief pitcher in the game's history.

As a high school kid in 1940, Hoyt learned to throw the knuckler by reading about it and studying pictures of the grips of the knuckler heroes of his boyhood. At the age of eighteen, in 1941, he got a job throwing it for Mooresville in the North Carolina State League. After three years in the Army, during which he won a Purple Heart in Germany, he returned to the minors and, mainly as a starter, won 107 games with his knuckler before it earned him his first major league job in 1952 with the New York Giants at the age of twenty-nine, when manager Leo Durocher pegged him as a relief specialist.

In his twenty-one-year odyssean career in both leagues—Giants, Cardinals, Indians, Orioles, White Sox, Angels, Braves, Cubs, and Dodgers—J. Hoyt Wilhelm became the best knuckleball pitcher ever, in the opinions of all the great hitters he baffled, and the only knuckler who threw it mainly as a reliever. He pitched only 2,254 innings in the 1,070 major league games (most ever) he was in, striking out 1,610 batters as against only 778 bases on balls. He won 143 games and lost 123. With 227 saves, he is listed as third among the relief specialists with 75 or more to their credit.

Hoyt pitched long, middle, and short relief, and a good many of his wins came with his team behind and in trouble, when he held off the opposing batters to give his team a chance to play catch-up and go-ahead offensive baseball.

As an uncomplaining reliever for the Giants and the St. Louis Cardinals, Hoyt yearned to start. His chance came in what he called his "darkest hour," when the Cardinals sold him in 1957 to the Cleveland Indians, who put him into their starting rotation in 1958. He won only three games for the Indians while losing seven. But Paul Richards, whom Hoyt described as "one of the most pitching-conscious managers in baseball," noted that most of the losses were by one run, and picked him up for $20,000 on August 23 of that season and gave him the ball as a starter for the Baltimore Orioles, laboring in sixth place. With Gus Triandos catching him with a special 38-inch mitt (designed by Richards), Hoyt could throw his knuckler harder and with more confidence.

His glory game came on September 20, 1958, when he knuckled the New York Yankees, bound for the World Series championship, for a 1–0 no-hit victory. Bases on balls to two batters, one of whom Gus threw out trying to steal second on a lazy floater, kept it from being a "perfect" game. Hoyt struck out eight, got six on ground balls, and retired the rest of the Bombers on pop-ups and routine flyballs. Gus, who hit his thirtieth home run of the season for the game's only score, said that catching Hoyt's knuckler that game was the hardest and best day's work he had ever put in.

In 1959, continuing as a starter, Hoyt renewed his mastery of Casey Stengel's champion Yankees. On April 22 he beat them in New York, 3–2. Then, in Baltimore on May 28, he almost had another no-hitter until it was spoiled by Jerry Lumpe's clean single in the eighth, and beat the Yanks 5–0, followed a few days later by another 5–0 win on four hits. But just as Babe Ruth was too mighty a hitter to play in only one of four games as a pitcher, Hoyt was too good an out-pitcher to be used only in the starting rotation. So it was back to the bullpen on behalf of Richards and the Orioles—and on to a total of 448 games in the National and 622 in the American League.

Wilhelm, a righthander, had two knucklers—one a "floater," the other a "spinner." He released both from a two-finger grip, letting the ball roll off the ends of his fore and long fingers. He threw the floater with a stiff wrist and no rotation. "The spinner breaks according to the way I rotate it," he said. "I try to make it turn one, sometimes two, times on the way to the plate. It breaks a lot more with two rotations than it does with one. If I release it sidearm, it will break out and laterally away from a righthanded batter. If I come down overhand or three-quarters with my motion, it will break down and out."

Since Wilhelm called it a thirty-year professional career at the age of forty-nine, Phil Niekro has taken his place as dean of the knuckleballers, and, forty-five years old as the 1984 season began, he may become the oldest man ever to pitch in the major leagues. A tribute to his knuckleball comes from George Hendrick of the Cardinals, one of the best hitters of contemporary times. When Phil was starting for the Atlanta Braves against the Cards, George preferred to warm the bench—not because he couldn't hit Phil's knucklers as well as or better than anybody else on the team, or because he was protecting his batting average, but because trying to time and hit them, he says, screwed up his swing for days at a time.

Unlike most knuckleballers, Hoyt Wilhelm could control his knuckler so well that he could work regularly in relief. *The Sporting News*

Ewell (The Whip) Blackwell's hopping-fast side-arm curve was good for one no-hit game and 8⅓ innings of another for the Cincinnati Reds in 1947. *The Sporting News*

Early Wynn won 300 major league baseball games, even though certain of his opponents knew which pitches he was about to throw. *The Sporting News*

Elroy Face of the
Pittsburgh Pi-
rates, master of
the forkball.
*The Sporting
News*

CHAPTER ELEVEN

The Forkball (Alias Bruce Sutter)

Nothing funny has ever been said about the forkball—except, perhaps, by Earl Weaver, the longtime Baltimore Orioles manager. While serving as a television commentator during the 1983 World Series, Weaver referred to the pitch that young Mike Boddicker used so well as a "foshball—half forkball and half dead fish."

Like the knuckler and other fancy deceivers, the forkball came into the majors when the legal spitter went out. By throwing it spinless (without pressure on the lower seams from the thumb and fourth finger), it can be make to look like a knuckler, but it is more difficult to throw, so there is not much incentive to learn to throw a forkball that looks like a knuckleball. Except on the sidelines and experimentally to relieve the boredom of the bullpen, the spinless version is rarely thrown in the majors, other than as a diversion with an 0–2 count and nobody on base.

The forkball can be thrown to look like a sharp down-breaking spitter—and there are fortunes to be made by those who can straddle the top seams with fore and long fingers, apply downspin with thumb and fourth finger, and throw it like a fastball with good control.

A great many pitchers have learned to throw and control the forkball as a favorite strikeout pitch, but most of them—Ernest (Tiny) Bonham of the New York Yankees in the thirties and forties, winding up with the Pittsburgh Pirates, is a good example—used it as a fourth pitch in their mix. Murry Dickson, when pitching for the Cardinals, Pirates, Phillies, Athletics, and Yankees, used it well as a seventh pitch (along with fastball, curve, slider, knuckler, screwball, a sinker, and a change-up variation of each). One reason that so few pitchers can make a bread-and-butter pitch out of it is that they do not have the long, strong fingers it takes to straddle the ball with proper release pressure. Elroy L. Face, who made it his specialty, developed the strength and suppleness of his big hand by working as a carpenter. (Murry Dickson was also a carpenter by off-season trade.) Bruce Sutter of the St. Louis Cardinals, another great forkball specialist, was born with fingers a full joint longer than normal and with an equally unusual strong and supple wrist.

Almost all of the great forkballers came into the major leagues with it as their best pitch. One who did not was Leslie Ambrose Bush. Breaking into the majors in 1912 with the Philadelphia Athletics, he earned his nickname, Bullet Joe, without it. In 1916, when he pitched a no-hitter against the Cleveland Indians, he lost 24 games, and in 1917 Connie Mack traded him to the Boston Red Sox for $60,000 and players. Still a fastballer, he went 15–15 for the Red Sox in 1918. After a year in the Army, he continued throwing bullets for Boston, with so-so success. Then at the age of twenty-nine he went to the Yankees in 1922 with "something else" in his repertory, a forkball, for a 26–7 season. That year he pitched 255 innings in 39 games and struck out only 92 batters while walking 85; batters were beating his forkball sinker into the ground for easy outs. Six seasons later, in 1928, he wound up his career back with the Athletics; used mainly in relief, he went out with a 2–1 record and a lifetime 195–182 mark.

Though Elroy Face began his brilliant career with Pittsburgh in 1953 primarily as a starting pitcher, his ability to throw strikes with his sinking forkball made him a sterling reliever. By 1956, when he started only 3 games and relieved in 65, he had become the premier fireman of his time. In the 802 games he pitched in for the Pirates (he is tied with Walter Johnson for most games pitched for one club), he started only 27 games and relieved in 775. In 1959 (before the statistical "saves" of 1969 and thereafter), he won 18 games and lost 1 in relief. When he ended his career with the Montreal Expos in 1969, he had a major league total of 1,375 innings pitched in 848 games, allowing 1,347 hits, only 362 bases on balls, and striking out 877 batters. Eight of the hits he gave up were grand slam home runs, one fewer than the record of nine held by several others.

The other great forkball pitcher is another reliever, Bruce Sutter, who came to the St. Louis Cardinals from the Chicago Cubs in a series of related trades that put both the Cardinals and Milwaukee Brewers into the 1982 World Series and made better ball clubs of both the Cubs and the Cardinals. Hub Kittle, the Redbirds' pitching coach then, hails Bruce as "the best forkball pitcher who ever pitched because nobody else has the God-given equipment to throw it like he does." As Hub sees it, the forkball is to Sutter what the fastball was to Walter Johnson, a sort of supernatural gift.

In Sutter's case it was a pair of gifts—abnormally long fingers and a slender wrist with the spring of a yew bow. The long fingers, whose spread and flexibility are enhanced by exercises that "Bruce is always fooling around with," enable him to grip the ball with less fork, or spread, than other forkballers, which is why Bruce calls it not a forkball at all but a "split-fingered fastball." He comes over the top with wrist-snap (like Johnson's) but no wrist-turn. His spread fingers are along the top seams and his thumb and fourth fingers grip the underside seams. "As he comes over and down with very fast arm action, just like his fastball," Hub says, "the ball squirts out with sinker spin from his thumb. The ball comes in looking like a straight fastball with a velocity around 85 miles an hour. As it gets to the plate, it just seems to sit, like an airplane coming in for a landing."

Batters, crouched to hit a low sinker at the bottom of the strike zone, frequently swing under the nonsinking fastball Sutter throws out of the same motion. Millions on television, with as good a view as he had of his own pitches, saw him get the final strikeout of the 1982 World Series with just such a rising fastball.

"That was exactly the type of spot they hired me for," said Sutter in the celebrating Cardinal clubhouse, speaking not only for himself but for all of the new breed of game-saving last-pitch relief specialists.

To get the Cardinals to their divisional championship that year, Sutter had 36 saves and 9 of the 92 Cardinal victories, which made him look cheap at his price—a million a year, or approximately $2,000 per forkball and another $500 each for the fastballs he sometimes throws in their stead.

Yankee Stadium, October 8, 1956: pitching from the stretch, Don Larsen comes in with the called third strike on Brooklyn's Dale Mitchell that concluded the only perfect game in World Series history. Billy Martin is the Yankee second baseman. *The Sporting News*

Don Drysdale of the Los Angeles Dodgers working against the San Francisco Giants' Chuck Hiller in the 1962 National League playoffs. The catcher is John Roseboro. *Associated Press*

Sandy Koufax's curve was said to make a perceptible sound as it came in toward the batter. *The Sporting News*

CHAPTER TWELVE

Out of the Blue

T hey said of Stu Miller, who came up with the St. Louis Cardinals in 1952, that he threw his variety of curves slow, slower, and slowest. Some said that the change-up of Walter (Boom Boom) Beck of the Phillies in the forties was the slowest, but Stan Musial, who batted against both, said that Stu's change-up on his change-up was a yard and a half slower than Boom Boom's. Miller and Beck are typical of so many curveball pitchers who have made respectable careers by changing speeds on their regular curves and thus also making such fastballs as they could occasionally muster seem "sneaky" fast. But they are change-up artists and do not belong in the category with those who have made a specialty of throwing those strange things called the slip pitch, palm ball, blooper, skyscraper, balloon, hesitation, and eephus, among the nonobscenities.

125

What these pitches, besides their honesty, have in common is that they come in slow and high over the batter's head and drop abruptly over the plate between the batter's armpits and knees without lateral curve. They are almost always thrown with a fastball (no wrist-turn) motion with backspin that causes them to rise in their zenith and then, like a well-hit wedge shot in golf, seem to come straight down on target. The palm ball and slip pitch, essentially the same, are held way back in the hand and slipped out, with even pressure, between thumb and little finger. How much the top fingers pull back determines the amount of backspin. If the top fingers are opened up at release, there is no spin, or very little, in which case the flight of the ball would be similar to a slow, high knuckler and would veer erratically and undependably, which is not the deceptive purpose of the pitch. Except for Satchel Paige's hesitation pitch and Rip Sewell's eephus ball—both of which are high-rotation pitches—the other names these pitches are called are descriptive of their flight, not of the technique used to throw them.

While such pitches undoubtedly go back to the early days of underhanded pitching, Paul Richards, as manager of the Baltimore Orioles, bears a large share of the responsibility for their elevation in the major leagues in the forties and fifties. The first slip pitch Richards ever saw, he recalled in 1958, was thrown by Fred (Deacon) Johnson in the Southern Association. "He didn't throw hard, and everybody thought they could hit him—until they tried. You would be up there waiting on this slow stuff, knowing he would come in with it. You would take a good strong cut, but the ball would seem to hesitate right around the plate, and you would be lucky to get a piece of it, usually for a pop-up." Richards, always fascinated by everything a ball could be made to do, could not beg or steal its secret from the Deak, who took it up with him to the St. Louis Browns.

When he was released, Richards, then managing Atlanta, claimed Johnson for use and further study, and while managing at Buffalo and Seattle in the minor leagues, began to get some of his pitchers to try to learn the Deak's slip pitch. It was not until 1951, when Richards was up with the Chicago White Sox, that Harry Dorish became the first of his pupils to master it. Later, at Baltimore, Jack Harshman, whom Richards rescued from the minor leagues, used it successfully, and so did Connie Johnson, who had learned it years before in the Negro leagues.

That is where Satchel Paige—who used it as a spectacular trick pitch in his prime, and later, finally in the majors as an old man, as a good "out" pitch—learned to throw his famous hesitation pitch. Cool Papa Bell told me that Satch learned it from William (Plunk) Drake of Sedalia, Missouri, who threw it for the old St. Louis Giants. As the preliminary to a trick pitch, Satch would take seven full windups before shoving off from his right foot. Then, while his right foot was coming down in follow-through, he would halt the downward motion of his arm and, Cool Papa said, "his arm would come down hard with it, but his hand would leave the ball behind, spinnin' up there in the sky all by itself."

Satch, who belongs in more pitching categories than anyone else, was 60 years, 2 months, and 18 days old when he threw the hesitation pitch for the last time in the major leagues, though he took it on several farewell exhibition tours to show folks how he used to strike out the best of them with it.

An even greater crowdpleaser—if only because he threw it through most of the 1940s before major league crowds—was Truett (Rip) Sewell's eephus pitch, also called his blooper. It was also—if only because he did not have all the other great stuff Satch threw—a more effective "out" pitch.

Although not nearly as long as it took Satch, of course, Rip needed quite a few years to establish himself as a major leaguer. After graduating from Alabama Military Institute, he got along in the minor leagues with a good, but not great, fastball and a "genuine slider" ("not the fast curve so many so-called slider pitchers are throwing today"), until, at twenty-five, he had an unsuccessful tryout with the Detroit Tigers in 1932. It was not until 1939 that he got out of the minors for good, began his twelve-year career with the Pittsburgh Pirates, and two years later introduced his eephus pitch.

Though he had been fooling around with it for several years, among the first major leaguers he showed it to was Alfonso Lopez, the great Hall of Fame catcher, also playing for Frankie Frisch and the Pirates. It was at their spring training camp in San Bernadino, California, in 1941. Throwing it on the sidelines, Rip would pull back on the top seams to give the ball as much backspin as he could out of his over-the-top fastball delivery. Al watched it soar 20 to 25 feet up, seem to hover, and come down fast into his mitt. "You've got to try it in a game, Rip." But Rip shook his head. "Frankie would never put up with a crazy pitch like that."

An irresistible opportunity came, while the club was heading east, in a preseason exhibition game in Muncie, Indiana, against the Detroit Tigers. Working the third inning allotted him, Rip had two runners on base when Steve O'Neill, Tiger manager, sent Dick Wakefield, a $100,000 bonus baby of monstrous size, in to bat. With regular stuff, Rip got two strikes on him. "So I figured this was my last chance to try it before the season opener, and I sent it up. He started to swing, stopped, started to swing again, stopped again, and it dropped past him for called strike three. Everybody hooted and hollered. The reporters came running to our bench to ask what I had thrown, 'I don't name it, I just throw it,' I told them. It was Maurice Van Robays, one of our players sitting on the bench beside me, who named it. 'It's a nothin' pitch,' he told the reporters, 'and eephus ain't nothin'.' "

I mentioned to Rip that I had seen it spelled epheus. "Maybe so. Maurice was born in Belgium. Maybe that's the way he learned to spell nothin'. But it came out eephus in all the papers. But after the opener in Chicago that year, a lot of people called it the blooper." (Van Robays's birthplace is actually listed as Detroit, Michigan.)

Its major league debut was a sensation. Rip went into the ninth leading the Cubs 1–0, but the Cubs loaded the bases with two out. Dominic Dallessandro, an outfielder, stood in and worked the count to three balls and two strikes. "Charlie Grimm was hollering to him to make sure the next pitch was in there. I set myself good and threw him the eephus. With everybody running, Dominic stood there like a soldier. It was strike three and our game. Dominic pointed his bat at me, and this is exactly what he said: 'You son of a bitch, if this was a rifle, I'd shoot you right between the eyes.' "

Part of the ensuing uproar came from baseball people who claimed that no such vertically falling pitch should ever be called a strike. A group of National League umpires went to Pittsburgh to watch as Rip pitched it to his teammates. As long as it crossed the plate between the letters and the knees, they decreed officially, they had no choice but to call it a strike.

It was good for business. In the Pirates' first trip to Sportsman's Park in St. Louis, the game Rip was to pitch had to be delayed half an hour to sell and take tickets from the unexpected throng that came to see his eephus pitch.

Rip's belated career seemed to be over that December when a shotgun blast in a hunting accident ripped into his right foot, shattering nearly every bone. He was told he would never be able to walk properly again, let alone pitch. He worked at learning to walk again and reported to spring training in San Bernadino, where he learned to pitch again. Because of stiffness in his foot and ankle, he had to toe the rubber with his right foot straight ahead instead of sideways on the edge of the rubber. This, he said, improved his control, because he "shoved off my right foot straight at the plate." Further, it made him a better fielding pitcher, because his follow-through took his right foot straight forward, and he was poised to go either way. In one game he had nine assists and a line drive comebacker putout. His eephus, his sneaky fast balls, and his "genuine slider," which he threw straight in with "a snap of my fingers that made it break," gave him fine years with the Pirates—including two 21-win seasons, the first in 1943 when he lost only 9, batted .286, and stole 10 bases. He played in the All-Star games of 1943, 1944, and 1946.

Sewell's own account of how Ted Williams hit the only home run off his eephus pitch was recorded by Tom McEwen of the Tampa *Tribune*, who went to see Rip, then a robust seventy-six, in his home in the Tampa area on the day of the 1983 All-Star game.

In the 1946 All-Star game in Fenway Park, the American League was leading the National League, 8–0, and the crowd was getting bored with the slaughter.

"Bill McKechnie and Charlie Grimm were managing the National League. They came to me and said, "Rip, you're going in there to wake this crowd up. Get warmed up.' I told them I didn't need no warm-up. I'd just shake hands with the catcher and that would warm me up.

"Snuffy Stirnweiss of the Yankees singled to left off me. Hal Wagner flew out but Jack Kramer, the pitcher, got another single. Sam Chapman scored Stirnweiss with a sacrifice flyball, and then Vern Stephens singled. So it was with two on that Ted Williams came up. He'd already hit a Kirby Higbe fastball nearly 500 feet out of the park. As he came to the plate, he looked out at me and said, 'Don't throw it.' I nodded my head and said, 'Yes, you're gonna get it.' The first one I threw was three inches outside. With his keen eye, he let it go. I threw him another one. He swung from Port Arthur and hit it foul over the National League dugout.

"He shook his head again. I nodded but slipped a fastball past him for one and two. He looked at me and shook his head again. I nodded yes, I was going to throw it. I threw him my Sunday blooper, my best one. He took three steps forward and hit it over that rightfield wall for a home run. He laughed all the way around the bases. It was the only home run ever hit off my eephus.

"Next batter was King Kong Keller of the Yankees. He was going to show the world he could do it, too. He swung with all his might and hit a pop about five feet in the air that Phil Masi, our catcher, almost dropped because he was laughin' so hard."

Describing his homer off Rip's eephus, Ted Williams said: "It came to the plate like a pop fly. It had a twenty-foot arc. Watching Rip warm up, I had said to Bill Dickey, 'I don't see how you could ever generate enough power to hit that pitch out of the park.' Dickey said the thing to do was to advance a step or two as it came toward you. Kind of run at it. That's what I did."

Rip pitched until 1949, retiring at forty-two after a pretty good 6–1 year. Still dauntless and full of wit and beans, he plays golf three times a week on artificial legs that replaced those he lost to the surgeon because of a blood circulation problem. He gets half-a-dozen letters and phone calls every day from fans like me who ask him fond but dumb questions, such as how come it became known as the eephus.

Whitey Ford, in 1964, as Yankee pitching coach. *The Sporting News*

Warren Spahn, who won more games than any other lefthanded pitcher in major league history, disdained the use of any trick pitches in his repertory. *Neils Lauritzen*

When his team finally realized that Wilbur Wood could throw his knuckler effortlessly all afternoon long, he became one of the game's most durable starting pitchers for the Chicago White Sox. *The Sporting News*

Lefty Steve Carlton, photographed back in 1971, when he still consented to talk to the press after winning ballgames. His sinker has made him one of baseball's all-time winning pitchers. *The Sporting News*

CHAPTER THIRTEEN

The Control Artists

"**S**atch didn't get in the majors by throwin' the ball over the plate. He made it by throwin' it over a matchbook on the edge of the plate."

At eighty, in his snug home in St. Louis—where the main problem he and his wife of 55 years, Clarabelle Bell, have is answering bags of fan mail and scheduling time for idolatrous reporters (like this one)—Cool Papa Bell, who talks as rapidly as he used to run the bases and shag flyballs, was telling how he helped Satchel Paige break into the majors with the Cleveland Indians.

It was in 1948, the year after Jackie Robinson cracked the color line. Cool Papa was then managing the second team of the Kansas City Monarchs, a breeding ground for young black players and a sanctuary for old ones. Satch, then only forty-three, was on his roster with a sore arm he had strained pitching winter ball for Caribbean

135

crowds after a full season of Negro ball and exhibition games from coast to coast.

Paige's God-given fastball was conjured away by the sudden appearance of a devilishly cool breeze that came off the briny while he was taking his ease, after pitching a game, on a warm and sunny beach in the Dominican Republic. It left him with "a cold in his arm." Neither ancient folk remedies and invocations nor modern medicine and the ministrations of specialists could summon back the lost spirit of his high hard one. Without it, he began barnstorming with a team of leftovers from the Kansas City Monarchs that Cool Papa Bell was coaching.

They were up in Iowa when Cool Papa got a phone call from Lou Boudreau, manager of the Cleveland Indians. With the color line gone for good, Lou wanted to know, as Cool Papa tells it, " 'Have you got any pitchers on the Monarchs who can throw strikes and help us win the pennant?' I told him the pitchers I had who can throw strikes don't have major league curves, except Old Satch."

Bill Veeck, Cleveland's general manager, who had prompted the original call, knew about Satchel Paige, of course—everybody in baseball did. His and Boudreau's concern, which they put to Cool Papa, was: "Ain't he too old?"

"What I told them," Cool Papa told me, "was these here very words. 'He can throw strikes without missing, and he's got a good curve and a new pitch to go with his sometimes fastball.' 'Bring him here,' they gave me the word that changed the world for Satch, 'and we'll take a look.' "

In Cleveland, Cool Papa put a matchbook on the plate to show Satch off. Over that matchbook, Satch threw 58 pitches for 54 strikes, and thereupon became the oldest rookie ever in the major leagues. Used mainly in relief—on the way to the pennant—Satch pitched 73 innings in 21 games, winning 6 and losing 1 with an ERA of 2.48; he struck out 45 and walked only 25 batters, some of the latter intentionally.

In the years before he needed his hesitation pitch and his assortment of curves, Satch had superb control of his blazing, moving fastball. One of his stunts in Negro and exhibition ball was to call in the outfielders (who would crouch behind the infielders) and strike out the side with nine fastballs, each zipping in precisely where he wanted it.

One of Satch's achievements, beyond the pale of the majors, was to make more money pitching than any major league pitcher of his time. He drew crowds of fans, black and white, wherever he was billed to pitch. Often, between scheduled starts for the Monarchs, he would pitch three innings to give his fans a look at him. His good right arm pitched in competition for forty years (1926–66). He was named to the Hall of Fame in 1971, three years before Cool Papa made it. No one doubts that his major league record, had he had one while in his prime, would have been celestial.

Of all the memorable control artists—Cy Young, Christy Mathewson, Charles (Deacon) Phillippe, Addie Joss, Carl Hubbell (among the two dozen who averaged less than two walks for every nine innings pitched over substantial careers)—the ailing and eccentric Grover Cleveland (Ol' Pete) Alexander takes the cake. Though few knew it, Pete was diabetic and epileptic.

He was unique because he did not have much going for him except control, pitching to batters' weaknesses during the latter part of his twenty years in the National League (1911–30). Neither his fastball nor his curve were outstanding as such by then, yet he never had to get around to developing "something extra." With his smooth, effortless delivery, he bent his curve and sneaked his fastball to precise spots where batters were most unlikely to make solid contact. His aim was to get the batter to hit the ball where it could be fielded for an out. "What's the use of doin' in three pitches what you can do in one?"

When, at twenty-four, he was just Pete, he set an all-time record by winning 28 games in his rookie year with the Philadelphia Phillies. He led the National League in most complete games for six seasons, in one of which (1916) he set another record by pitching 16 shutouts. By economizing on the number of pitches he threw, he pitched and won doubleheaders in 1916 and 1917. He wound up his career with 373 games won (tied with Mathewson) and an ERA of 2.56, second only to Johnson's 2.37. In the 5,188 innings he pitched for the Phillies, Cubs, and Cardinals, he struck out 2,198 batters and walked only 953—1.66 walks for every nine innings pitched. It was Ol' Pete and Herb Pennock, another control artist who was winding up his great Yankee career, who inspired Marse Joe McCarthy's dictum that a pitcher with unfailing control was the best bet in a jam.

Rogers Hornsby, manager of the Cardinals, thought so, too, in the seventh inning of the seventh game of the 1926 World Series against the Yankees. Ol' Pete was snoozing off the effects of a hangover he had earned by winning the sixth game the day before. But he was roused to respond to Hornsby's summons to the mound. Before handing him the ball, Hornsby made certain Ol' Pete (then nearly forty) understood the game situation. St. Louis had a 3–2 lead. The bases were loaded. There were two out. "That's Tony Lazzeri standing in," Hornsby told him.

Ol' Pete looked around, nodded, and took the ball. "I guess there ain't no place to put him, is there?"

Without taking a warm-up pitch, he went to work and struck out Lazzeri with a low curve on the corner. He stayed in the game to hold the lead as the Cardinals won the world championship.

Christy Mathewson's career disputes the notion, expressed by many, that control, like the velocity of a fastball, is innate. Sent home after his rookie tryout (with the suggestion that he might make an acceptable first baseman), he spent hours throwing balls at and through a four-inch slit in his father's barn wall. That kind of solitary practice, boy and man, is an old sweet song from the earliest days of the game. Christy issued only 1.56 walks for each nine of the 4,781 innings he pitched in the majors.

Control, though, cannot be measured by walks alone. Some of the best pitchers of all time are leaders in bases on balls—including such disparate artists in different eras as Walter Johnson, Burleigh Grimes, Bobby Feller, Warren Spahn, Buck Newsom, Bob Gibson, Red Ruffing, and Amos Rusie, all of whom walked 1,200 or more batters.

In addition to the continuing competition for most career strikeouts between Nolan Ryan and Steve Carlton, both are also in contention for most walks, although it seems likely that Nolan may become the first major league pitcher ever to exceed 2,000.

Walks may not be so much a measure of wildness as of confidence and cunning. Because control pitchers know they can make the ball do and go as they want it to, they often challenge batters with their best stuff—up or down, in or away—instead of aiming lollipops into the strike zone.

And real or feigned wildness is an everyday—or a career-long—tool of intimidation for many a fastballer. Bob Feller, who walked 1,764 batters, made good use of his reputation for wildness in keeping batters loose. But even as a wild kid in his rookie year in 1936, he was the winner of a control contest before 65,000 fans in Cleveland. Before the game, a square target about the size of an ordinary picture frame was hung over the plate, and pitchers of both teams vied at throwing the best of five pitches through it. When Feller, the last to try, went to the mound, the leader was George Uhle (then with Cleveland, winding up a seventeen-year career in which he had walked only 960 batters) with two for five. The wild kid fired all five through the target, and the crowd cheered for five minutes.

Gaylord Perry, who concluded an illustrious twenty-two-year major league pitching career in 1983, is one of only two pitchers since 1920 to have been ejected from a game for throwing a spit-ball. Note that the grip in this photo is remark-ably like that used for throwing the wet one. *The Sporting News*

A family of knuckleballing brothers, both of whom have been consistent winners for many years: Joe, *left*, and Phil Niekro.

The Sporting News

Malcolm W. Emmons

Don Sutton, one
of baseball's top
pitchers, is re-
ported to bear the
nickname of
"Black and
Decker" because
of his skillful em-
ployment of cer-
tain tools of his
trade. *Malcolm
W. Emmons*

CHAPTER FOURTEEN

The Once Honest, But for Long Crooked, Spitter and Its Various Nefarious Cousins

The kimono ball is the only new pitch introduced to baseball during the latter half of this century, and it died in its debut.

Its sponsor and inventor was Tommy Byrne, a New York Yankee lefthander known for his high humor and his high hard one. He is credited with being first to throw an inside pitch while hollering, "Watch it!" He invented the kimono ball in 1955 while on one of the early postseason exhibition tours of Japan that helped foment interest in baseball there to a hysteria matched only by that in the Americas. His original aim was, he said, to entertain Japanese fans and to give Japanese players something else to imitate. From a set position, looking in, he would take his arm back normally and, while striding forward, continue a backward swing and deliver the ball from behind his back. He got so he could control it pretty well. While it did not have much velocity and only a slight rainbow drop, its charm was that it came to batters who were expecting to see it coming toward them from one side, the meanwhile it was still revolving around his back.

Byrne took it to spring training and showed it to Casey Stengel. Recognizing it as something new under the baseball sun, the sage Yankee manager gave Tommy permission to fling it in a preseason exhibition game. Tommy unveiled it on Sunday, March 26, 1956, in a game in Miami against the Brooklyn Dodgers. The batter, Pee Wee Reese, was too surprised to swing. Whether it was in the strike zone or not is not a matter of record, because the umpire, Larry Napp of the American League, called it a "discard" pitch and told Tommy not to throw it again.

Though thrown only once, the kimono ball and its implications were discussed in every dugout and in the high chambers of officialdom. The most important thing said about it was the dictum of Cal Hubbard, chief of American League umpires, that it was illegal and would not be permitted. Pee Wee Reese called it a "bush" pitch that gave the fans and his teammates a good laugh. Other players, citing the need for more humor in the game, argued for its legality. Speaking for many, Mickey Owen, then a Dodger coach, said : "Tommy's a lefthander, ain't he? Then he's entitled to do those things. There ought to be more of this kind of stuff in baseball."

Hearing about it, Ted Williams agreed that the kimono pitch should be made legal, but for a different reason: "I could add it to the collection of funny pitches I have hit for home runs."

Casey Stengel held an informal press conference about it. Without lamenting its illegality, he said it was the only new pitch he had seen since the sophisticated slider evolved from the nickel curve.

"Will there ever be another really new pitch?" he was asked.

Ol' Case thought back through his fifty years in baseball and shook his head. "I see nothing new in the offing—except, maybe, a new variation of the slider and new ways to get by with all the old crooked stuff we know about. I wish," he added wistfully, "that somebody would invent a control ball with which it would be impossible to give a base on balls."

Baseball is nobler and less hypocritical than other endeavors because it countenances and even honors illegal deceptions. Crookery and cheating in business, politics, cards, and courtship, though rampant and profitable, disgrace those who get caught; but in professional baseball, seeking, finding, and using an illegal edge is a prideful achievement. The only resolution that getting caught cheating inspires is not to get caught again—a matter of personal chagrin, not public disgrace.

The kimono ball was unique in that it is the only pitch declared illegal in this century because of its delivery motion. Within the bounds of foot position and movement, the required set position, and balk infringements, none of which the kimono ball violated, a pitcher can legally throw the ball any other way he can get it from mound to plate.

Illegal pitches are thrown properly, but with balls whose surfaces or innards have been craftily changed to cause abnormal flight. Surface changes, easy to make and get away with, are used almost exclusively to accomplish this, but cunning pitchers and managers have not neglected the ball's interior, either. The rumor about Ted Lyons, a Hall of Famer who pitched for the Chicago White Sox from 1923 to 1946 (except for three years of World War II military service), was that he opened balls and stuffed them with Mexican jumping beans: such was the only plausible explanation for his erratic stuff. It is a fact that league offices several times have called in strangely behaving balls and sawed them in half to look for interior alterations.

The most venerable and common way to change balls inwardly was to freeze or heat them before delivering them to the umpires. The frozen ball was dead, while the oven ball would turn a flyball into a towering homer. The trick was to get the frozen balls into the hands of your pitchers, and the oven balls to theirs—a feat for which John McGraw and his Baltimore Orioles of yesteryear became notorious.

In 1954, Johnny Cooney, then pitching coach for the Milwaukee Braves, recalled the pride he felt in 1923 after shutting out the Philadelphia Phillies on two scratch hits, only to learn two years later from a private confession by Art Fletcher of the Phillies that he had done it with frozen balls planted with the plate umpire by the Phillies: "We only got four hits but squeezed in a run to beat them with their own dead balls," Johnny recalled, adding that under present procedures he doubted a team could foist frozen balls on umpires. Johnny didn't know about today's deep freezers that make it possible for the core of a ball to remain frozen long after its surface warms up—and give a team of swifty singles hitters a field day against lumbering power-hitting opponents. A fair assumption in baseball is that if it can be done, it is being done.

Whether it was coincidence or part of the fervor of a majority of Americans to curtail the bad habits and evil practices of others—the war to "make the world safe for democracy" had just been won—is beyond this purview, but it is a fact that making and selling booze with more than one-tenth of one percent alcoholic content and pitching baseballs with personality-changing additives and defacements were both voted illegal in 1919, to become effective in 1920. While both bannings made life more difficult for the law-abiding and more lush for the crooks, neither resulted in any substantial reduction in usage. The Eighteenth Amendment went down the drain fifteen years later as the Noble Experiment that failed, but major league baseball has persisted in its mostly futile efforts to identify, detect, and enforce its ban in the pitching of altered baseballs.

Though amended and interpreted over the years, Rule 8.02 of 1919 is still in the game's constitution:

The pitcher shall not: (1) apply a foreign substance of any kind to the ball or his glove; (2) expectorate either on the ball or his glove; (3) deface the ball in any manner; (4) deliver what is called the "shine" ball, "spit" ball, "mud" ball, or "emery" ball. The pitcher, of course, is allowed to rub the ball between his bare hands.

And, ay, there's the rub that makes it easy to "load" or deface a ball without getting caught doing it.

One of the chief amendments, enacted in 1968, recognizes that the importance of their work with respect to winning or losing baseball games tends to make pitchers nervous and fidgety people. While it forbids the pitcher from bringing his pitching hand "in contact with his mouth or lips while in the 18-foot circle surrounding the pitching rubber," the amendment does not forbid him from doing so while off the mound between pitches. There he can "go to his mouth," blow on his hands, scratch his nose or any other itchy part of his anatomy, tug at his anatomy, tug at his uniform, wipe honest sweat off his brow or the back of his neck, adjust his cap, and perform other habitual rituals before returning to the mound to signal his catcher that he is coming in with a wet one.

Having fidgeted, however, he must dry his fingers, usually by tossing the rosin bag, before rubbing or turning the ball to set his grip. It is up to the umpires to see that he dries them, but this is often an impossible observation to make. Suppose, for example, he deposits a glob of slippery saliva on his fingernails and puts on a good show of drying their inside tips? He can make the transfer while exercising his right to rub the ball between his bare hands.

Another amendment forbids the pitcher to "have on his person or in his possession" any slippery substance or anything with which to scuff or gouge the surface of the ball. To enforce this section of 8.02, the umpires are authorized to make a search and, if they find forbidden surface-changers, immediately to eject the pitcher from the game. To look into every area of concealment would require the equivalent of a police strip-search, so umpires use their inspection authority reluctantly and rarely.

For a few years after the 1967–68 interpretations and amendments—which made the umpire "the sole judge" and gave him responsibility for detecting violations and enforcing penalties—umpires were more diligent in using their search authority than has been true in recent years. A pivotal case was that of Phil Regan, a late-inning relief pitcher for the Chicago Cubs, whose wicked sinker, umpires and opposing players alike believed, could only be achieved with the use of a "foreign substance" on his fingers or the ball. He was searched fruitlessly several times in 1968 and 1969. Some of his pitches were called balls when umpires exercised their right to call an illegality on the basis of their judgment of the flight of the ball. One of his pitches, hit for an easy flyball out, was called a "no pitch" because, in the umpire's judgment, it came in like a "loaded" pitch.

On May 7, 1970, when Regan came to the mound to pitch in the eighth inning against the Cincinnati Reds, he was frisked by umpire Chris Pelekoudas, who checked his hands, arms, cap, glove, pants, and shirt and ran his fingers through his hair to see if more oil was present than decent grooming would require. Finding nothing, Pelekoudas stopped the game to inspect the ball after every suspicious pitch, the Wrigley Field fans booing and hooting at the delays. Regan, who protected the lead, complained about it after the game.

"I realize it's the umpire's job to come out and check me out," he said, "but when they find nothing, that should be it. I don't believe they should be allowed to stop the game repeatedly to look at the ball. That becomes harassment." Then, smiling at an afterthought, he admitted that, "if it doesn't go too far, there's an advantage, because when batters get to wondering what I'm going to throw, they can't concentrate on what I am throwing."

Don Drysdale, who wound up his brilliant fourteen-year career with the Los Angeles Dodgers in 1969 and who is believed to have achieved a good many key strikeouts with slick-spotted balls while on the way to a career earned-run average of 2.95, said he would not stand for a search on the mound. "It would have to be a private showing in the dugout. Besides," he added, "when I have fingers run through my hair, I usually get kissed." Another Dodger, Don Sutton, though, said if he were to be searched, he would insist upon being stripped to his shorts, right out in front of God, the television audience, and the paying customers.

In any event, after Warren Giles, the National League president, looked into the Regan case—including charges that he was being unfairly "persecuted" by umpires—he reported no findings of illegality on the part of Regan. Though no policy statement on searches was issued, they have not been nearly so diligently conducted since that time.

An important reason, though not one publicly stated, for the reluctance of umpires to call pitching illegalities and to enforce penalties is the possibility of damage suits brought by pitchers for deprivation of livelihood. With today's top salaries of a million or more a year, such claims could run, as they say, into real money even without punitive penalties. And who is to assure an umpire and his bosses that a jury would not award them? Such "hard evidence" as scuffs or remnants of hair tonic on the ball allegedly thrown would be challenged as accidental, or applied after confiscation. Expert witnesses by the dozen could swear on the Bible that the flight of an illegal spitter or scuffball is indistinguishable from that of a sinking forkball or a sharp-breaking slider, so help them God.

Only in regard to the beanball does Rule 8.02 raise the question of the ethics of illegal pitches. To "intentionally pitch at the batter" is both illegal and, as a note to the rule states, "unsportsmanlike and highly dangerous. It should be—and is—condemned by everybody." That is why—although the umpire must make a judgment call on whether a pitch "got away" inadvertently or was aimed at a batter out of meanness or retaliation—beanball calls are less troublesome and controversial than those based upon real or suspected tampering with the surface of the ball. Society does not approve of the beanball. Otherwise, anything goes.

There are a hundred names for different ways to doctor a ball—to change its personality—and the nomenclature of malpractice changes with advances in the state of the art. But they all derive—with the exception of such internally induced psychoses as the frozen and the Mexican Jumping Bean balls—from the four generic flight-changers outlawed by rule 8.02. Going from least to most used, they are the "mud," the "shine," the "emery," and the "spit." Let us examine them in that order.

THE MUD BALL

In the generic mud ball, an imbalance, or lopsidedness, is created by weighting a seamline with mud, beeswax, fine cinders, old-fashioned steel phonograph needles or small nails, or ATW—anything that works. The charm of the mud ball is that it gives more action to every pitch. Usually thrown as a curve, the ball responds with greater alacrity to the spin put on it, though sooner and wider and often without a sharp break near the plate. The use of the mud and other such variants increases the initial swerve of the knuckler and other spinless pitches, but, as the weighted seam tilts down and stabilizes the fluctuation of the seams, it tends to come to the plate on an even course, like a boat with a fixed sail. However thrown, the deception of the mud ball lies in the fact that it does not behave like other doctored balls thrown the same way.

The shortcomings of the mud ball lie in the fact that it is more difficult to create without detection, and also to control the amount and nature of its action, than either the emery or spit balls. The reason it is now mainly a memory is that there are more reliable ways to doctor a ball and fool batters. If they still needed the mud ball, pitchers would be finding new techniques and substances to use—if only on the assumption that if it is illegal, it must work. Come to think of it, anybody could go to any hardware store and buy tubes of cements and fillers of adequate density that dry quickly and invisibly.

THE SHINE BALL

The shine ball is one that is smoother and slicker on one surface than on the others. Decreased air resistance on the slick side causes the ball, thrown like a fastball, to curve in the direction of less pressure.

In the old days, licorice, tobacco, and slippery elm saliva were favorite agents. In addition to its extra action, an old-fashioned shine ball—one side dark and the other white—was a visual distraction to the batter, especially when coming out of deep shade on the mound or going into a shade-enshrouded plate area. Today's favorites are such slick and colorless potions as metamucil-slick saliva, hair tonic, and vaginal cream. "Smell it! Smell it!" demanded Billy Martin, then manager at Oakland, thrusting an exotically treated ball at an umpire, who raised his nose and shook his head. "Now," Billy complained, "I got an umpire who can't smell or see!"

The "pure" shine ball is still thrown, mainly to give extra veer or hop to a fastball, but its principal use now is as an adjunct to the spitball. As the size of the slick surface used to reduce finger friction on the spitball is increased, the amount of shine effect on the ball is also increased. This is why many spitballs veer laterally as they sink at the plate, often as much to the pitcher's surprise as to the batter's chagrin.

THE EMERY BALL

The effect of emery is opposite that of shine. One surface is roughened or gouged to increase air resistance on that side. Now generally known as the scuffball, it is the easiest crooked pitch to throw and control—and because it is easy on the arm, perhaps the most effortless pitch of all, whether honest or crooked. This is because it can be—and usually is—thrown like a warm-up fastball, without wrist-turn. The scuff or gouges on the ball create action that would otherwise come only from an arm-straining delivery.

In the May, 1981, issue of *Inside Sports*, Thomas Boswell reported an illuminating demonstration of the scuffball given him by Mike Flanagan, the Oriole lefthander who was the Cy Young Award winner in 1979. Mike made three inch-long gouges on the surface of a new ball, explaining that they were more excessive than a skillful scuffballer would require. By gripping the ball with the scuffed side opposite to the break, he threw pitches that broke in, out, up, and down. "It takes no talent whatsoever," he told his Boswell. "You just throw it like a mediocre fastball. The scuff gives the break. . . . A good scuffballer can throw a ball a third as hard and make the ball move twice as much as an honest pitcher."

Mike, of course, insisted that he had never thrown a scuffball in a game—nor the "pretty good bullpen spitter" he had developed, either.

It is as easy to scuff a ball as it is to throw one. However, once created, the scuff or gouge is on the ball to stay. Unlike saliva or slick lotions that are obscured when a ball is hit on the ground or in the air, fielded, handled, and thrown, or removed when the pitcher rubs a returned ball before pitching it again, the scuff is there to be seen by foe or umpire. But it is surprisingly difficult to prove when, how, and by what or whom the scuff was made, and whether accidentally or deliberately. A pitcher can do it with a bit of concealed sandpaper, a sharpened belt buckle, or any of several other tools and devices. Calling for a suspected ball, the umpire can and does throw scuffed balls out of the game, but unless he gets two or three balls that have been scuffed or gouged identically, there is little he can do except to warn the pitcher and echo the complaints of the batters.

Of the countless thousands of "emery" or scuffballs which have been thrown in the majors since they were banned nearly sixty-five years ago, only those thrown by one pitcher—Rick Honeycutt, pitching in 1980 for the Seattle Mariners—were judged flagrant enough to get him ejected, suspended, and fined. (Since 1920 only two pitchers—Nelson Potter of the St. Louis Browns in 1944 and Gaylord Perry of the Mariners in 1982—have been ejected, suspended, and fined for throwing spitters.) Honeycutt was caught orange-handed, you could say, by Bill Kunkel, who had been a pitcher and a confessed spitball thrower himself before he joined the forces of law and order and became an umpire.

Before Honeycutt went to the mound to start the game, the opposing Kansas City Royals asked Kunkel to check the balls following any and all dippy sinkers and unnatural curves. In the first two innings he set aside, as evidence, two balls, each with three identical slashes. In the third inning he got a third ball that was slashed just like the others. With Hal McRae at bat, Kunkel went to the mound and noticed an orange (flesh)-colored adhesive bandage on the index finger of Honeycutt's glove hand. He grabbed the band and noted the presence of a thumbtack sticking up through the bandage. "So," he said, "take a walk."

McRae, who had stepped out to watch, meanwhile picked up a piece of coarse sandpaper he had seen fall out of Honeycutt's glove. "Here," he said, handing it to Kunkel, "you might as well get the whole kit." Honeycutt was, as Kunkel reported it, "both cutting it and scuffing it, depending on what he wanted the ball to do."

Along with the ten-day suspension, the most painful punishment Honeycutt suffered was the jeers of his peers for being clumsy about it.

There is nothing clumsy about Don Sutton's handiwork on a baseball. Nearing forty, making close to a million dollars a year, and nearing the 275 career victory mark in the majors, Don answers to the nickname "Black and Decker," hung on him because of the tools and devices he is supposed to keep handy while near the mound or on it. A bit of dialogue he had with plate umpire Don Denkinger in the game he pitched for the Milwaukee Brewers which won the American League championship in 1982 is illustrative of Don's cynical charm. "Somehow," he said contentedly in the clubhouse after the 10–2 drubbing of the Orioles, "a mysteriously scuffed ball got into the game. Denkinger told me that if I found another like it, he would appreciate it if I would throw it out of the game. I said I would be happy to oblige. I did find one and threw it out. I don't like them in the game. It would be too hard to throw them straight."

He threw the key pitch of the game in the fifth inning when the Orioles, down only 3–1, loaded the bases with two out and had Eddie Murray, their most productive batter, standing in. Sutton, a righthander, got him out on a grounder with a pitch that broke up and away from the lefthanded batter.

"What did you get him with?" he was asked.

"Oh, that?" Don said. "That pitch? That was my tailing fastball."

Ray Miller, the Orioles' pitching coach, whose own illegal specialty as a pitcher was the spitter, said that he believed Sutton's "fine example of defiance" of the rules against scuffing would inspire other pitchers to go, thou, and do likewise. "Someday," Ray said, "I expect to see a pitcher walk out to the mound with a utility belt on—file, chisel, screwdriver, glue. . . . He'll throw a ball to the plate with bolts attached to it."

The simplified enforcement procedures adopted in 1980 would seem to make Ray's prediction farfetched. Under them, the umpire sees that the pitcher starts each inning with an unscuffed ball, and the pitcher is responsible for the purity of each ball he throws. If the umpire finds a scuffed ball, he can search the pitcher, or warn him, or both, keeping the ball as evidence. Upon finding another, similarly scuffed or gouged, he is to eject the pitcher for an automatic ten-day suspension. What could be a more pitcher-proof procedure than that? And yet—which is probably what Ray had in mind about inspirational defiance of the rules—there is bare, shining fact that for more than sixty years, only Rick Honeycutt has paid the price for throwing an "emery" ball.

In his sixteen years (1950, 1953–67) of glory as a Yankee pitcher, Edward (Whitey) Ford accumulated eleven World Series rings. I wonder whether, in a special place among them, he keeps the steel ring, its bottom harshly rasped, that, along with a judicious spitter and his brilliant assortment of honest curves and fastballs, allegedly helped him to a career earned-run average of 2.74 and entry into the Hall of Fame at Cooperstown?

THE SPITTER

The "spit" ball has the most superlatives attached to it of the four kinds of tampered balls forbidden by rule 8.02. It is the most esteemed and most despised of the crooked pitches, the most controversial, the most effective, the least detectable, the most widely used, and the most difficult to master. Whether it is hard or easy on a pitching arm is one of its most controversial aspects.

While the first wet one—aka, vaselineball, greaseball, jellyball, slicker, etc., but usually, generically, the spitter—was undoubtedly thrown back in the early years of the game with a rain- or puddle-wet ball, perhaps by little Bobby Matthews of Baltimore (as Phoney Martin attested), its emergence as a major league pitch is credited to George Hildebrand, who was not himself a pitcher.

As with most "firsts" of the game, you will find gainsayers who assert otherwise, but Hildebrand's story, related as an elder statesman in 1955, is consistent with and corroborated by those of the other early explorers of its deceptive flight to the plate. In 1902, playing outfield for Providence, Hildebrand warmed up before a game with Frank (Fiddler) Corridon, a rookie pitcher. He noticed that Frank would wet the tips of his fingers before throwing his change-up, a nearly spinless blooper.

"Kidding," George said, "I took the ball and put a big daub of spit on it and threw it in to Brown, who was catching. It took such a peculiar shoot that all of three of us noticed it." Brown told him to cut it out. Corridon, however, asked him how he did it, and Hildebrand showed him, coming down hard with an overhanded pitch. Four weeks later, in an exhibition game against Pittsburgh, Corridon used the Hildebrand version of the spitball to strike out nine batters in five innings, "and then couldn't raise his arm, so he had to be taken out."

Hildebrand finished that season with Sacramento in the Pacific Coast

League, where a teammate was Elmer Stricklett, a pitcher who had a sore arm and was about to be released. "Guess I'm about through," he conceded to Hildebrand.

"Let me show you something," Hildebrand said, and "gave him the secret of what we called the wet one."

Stricklett practiced with it for four days, won eleven straight games, kept his job, pitched two more years for Sacramento, and then took it east to the majors.

In corroboration of Hildebrand's story, Stricklett stated that "the first fellow to use the spitball was Frank Corridon. Hildebrand brought it to the Coast in 1902 and showed it to me." Hildebrand retired as a player in 1913 and continued in the game as an American League umpire until 1934.

From its Corridon-Hildebrand-Stricklett origin, the spitter soon became an "out pitch" in the repertory of many pitchers who needed "something else" to win games and who could master it without hurting their arms. It was meat-on-the-table to so many pitchers that, when rule 8.02 outlawed it in 1920, exceptions were granted to eight National League and nine American League pitchers, all certified by their clubs as bona fide spitballers. Alphabetically, with their sponsoring clubs and the last year each pitched in the majors, the National Leaguers were: Bill Doak, Cardinals, 1929; Phil Douglas, Giants, 1922; Dana Fillingim, Braves, 1925; Ray Fisher, Reds, 1920; Marvin Goodwin, Cardinals, 1925; Burleigh Grimes, Dodgers, 1934; Clarence Mitchell, Dodgers, 1932; and Dick Rudolph, Braves, 1927.

In the American League: Y. A. (Doc) Ayers, Tigers, 1921; Ray Caldwell, Indians, 1921; Stanley Coveleski, Indians, 1928; Urban (Red) Faber, White Sox, 1933; H. S. (Dutch) Leonard*, Tigers, 1925; John Picus Quinn, Yankees, 1933; Allen Russell, Red Sox, 1925; Urban Shocker, Browns, 1928; and Allen Sothoron, Browns, 1926.

Of the lot, three—Coveleski, Faber, and Grimes—spat their way into the Hall of Fame. In his fourteen years in the majors, winding up with the New York Yankees in 1928 at age thirty-eight, Stan Coveleski had the lowest earned-run average of any of the legal spitballers—2.88, while winning 215 games. He was one of four brothers who played professional baseball—the others were Frank and John in the minors, and Harry, who had a good ten-year pitching career with the Phillies, Reds, and Tigers.

---

*This Dutch Leonard finished his career almost ten years before the better known Emil (Dutch) Leonard began his twenty-year (1933–53) major league career.

Red Faber, who won 254 games in the twenty years he pitched for the Chicago White Sox, pitched four games and beat the Giants in three of them in the World Series of 1917, when the Sox won the world championship. He was forty-five years old when he pitched his last professional spitter in 1933. Quinn, known as Picus, was the oldest of the group to throw a legal spitter in the majors. He was forty-nine when, in 1933, he finished a twenty-year career in the majors while pitching for the Cincinnati Reds. He stayed in professional baseball, however, for another two years and was fifty-one when he threw his last spitter for Johnstown in the Mid-Atlantic League. Starting out with Macon in the South Atlantic League in 1907, Quinn pitched professionally for twenty-eight years.

Uninhibited by the nuisance of surreptitious application, it was Burleigh Arland (Old Stubblebeard) Grimes who was the great star of the legal spitballers and also belongs in the more select group of the most distinguished pitchers of all time. He got his start in professional ball at nineteen with Eau Claire in the Minnesota-Wisconsin League, not far from his birthplace and boyhood home in Emerald, Wisconsin. After four years in the minors, he began his nineteen-year major league career in 1916 with the Pittsburgh Pirates. His longest stint with a single club was in Ebbets Field, during the nine years (1918–26) when he was one of the Beloved Bums of Brooklyn—or Dem Bums as dey was called by sportswriters during the Durocher era. Grimes's best year for the Dodgers was his first year as a legal spitballer. In 1920 he led the National League with 23 wins against 11 losses, and an earned-run average of 2.22. In 1927, his only year with the New York Giants, he won 13 consecutive games. The next year, back with the Pirates, was the best of his career. He pitched 331 innings in 48 games and won 25 of them, with 14 losses and an earned-run average of 2.99—this at a time when earned runs were moving toward an all-time high in 1929 and 1930.

Burleigh's greatest public acclaim came in 1931, as a member of the St. Louis Cardinals. By then the proliferation of radio sets was bringing live accounts of ball games to most homes and to every hamlet in the land. As what was then the farthest south and most western of any major league team, the Cardinals were the favorites of the largest spread, geographically, of baseball fans in the world. Grimes won 17 games for them on their way to the pennant, and, more dramatically, with millions listening in, won two of the four games that the underdog Cardinals took from the mighty Philadelphia Athletics to win the world championship. In those two victories, he gave up only four runs for a 2.04 earned-run average. After two subsequent years with St. Louis, Chicago, and Pittsburgh, he played out his string for the New York Yankees in 1934, the last (but not, at forty-one, the oldest) of the legal spitballers.

A seeming paradox of baseball, noted previously, is that Burleigh Grimes and others of the greatest pitchers in the game had so much confidence in their control that they walked numerous batters. They were always flirting with the corners, up or down. Even with a three-ball, two-strike count, they would try to pitch to a spot instead of aiming the ball toward the middle of the strike zone. Confident of getting the next batter anyway, they figured that the base on balls they might give up was a better gamble than a likely hit, perhaps for extra bases, off a pitch delivered down main street. Burleigh walked a total of 1,295 batters, putting him in the over-1,200 class along with Early Wynn, Allie Reynolds, Warren Spahn, Bob Gibson, Nolan Ryan (the leader with 1,921, entering the 1983 season), Phil Niekro, and Gaylord Perry.

Unlike them, however, Burleigh was not also among the leaders in strikeouts, of which he had only 1,512, about one-half as many as Walter Johnson. Part of the reason for his durability was that like Ol' Pete Alexander, he saved wear on his arm by obliging batters to take corner pitches for strikes or swing at balls they could not hit solidly.

He could throw strikes with his spitter when a walk could lose a game. Once, with the bases loaded and the tying run on third with two out in a game between his Dodgers and the Chicago Cubs, he was called to the mound in the ninth inning to get the final out and save the game. He aimed three pitches wide of the strike zone. Knowing the batter was hoping for a game-winning walk, he thereupon threw two fast balls in for called strikes. "Then," he said, recalling the fun of it, "I snapped off the spitter, and that was that. I actually struck the guy out on one pitch."

Like almost all great spitballers, Burleigh threw his with the same motion and no-turn wrist of his fastball. He chewed slippery elm, described as "a mucilaginous demulcent made from the fragrant inner bark of the North American elm," used by American Indians as a scurvy preventive, and which Burleigh found "tasty, really delicious," to produce the slippery spit he applied generously to the ball, making a spot about the size of a fifty-cent piece.

To make the ball drop sharply at the plate, he would let his first and second fingers slip frictionless off the slippery elm while creating downspin with the grip of his thumb and other fingers on the lower seams. He could also make the ball break away from a righthanded batter or sail up and in at a lefty.

Long years after his retirement as a pitcher, while a scout for the Baltimore Orioles in 1961, he explained: "To make a ball break down, I would throw it like an overhanded fastball. To make it break to the left, I would throw it sidearm. Any angle between overhand or sidearm, I would get that angle of break on the ball."

"I never tried to guess on his spitter," said Frank Frisch, the Hall of Fame infielder who played both against and with Burleigh. As a switch-hitter batting lefthanded against Grimes, he found that "It broke just one way—in toward my head. I did more spitting—spitting out dirt—than he ever did."

Throwing it was easy on his arm, Burleigh said, because he threw it with his arm fully extended. The strain of throwing the pitch with a crook in the elbow, he thought, was the reason for sore-arm spitballers. "It's not hard to learn the basic facts of throwing the spitball, but it can't be taught to just anyone in ten pitches," he said. "It's really an art because it's a difficult pitch to control. But once it's perfected, you've added a real weapon to the pitches you've got."

Burleigh added it to his repertory as a teenager after seeing it in action in the first professional game he ever saw. "I went to see Henry Gehring in the old Lexington Avenue ballpark in St. Paul in 1909 when he was pitching for the Saints against the Toledo Mudhens. With the help of my uncle, who played ball, I worked on it for four or five years. Then, at my own expense, I went to Eau Claire for a tryout, and the spitball helped get me my first start in professional ball."

But another spitballer of that era may have been an even greater master of the pitch than Old Stubblebeard. Through an oversight by the Chicago White Sox—or, as some more kindly put it, because of a rule interpretation—Frank Shellenback was not included on the 1920 major league list of legal spitballers. Frank broke in with Providence in 1917. His brief major league pitching career with the White Sox was in 1918–19, pitching in 36 games. Either his major league career was deemed insufficient or else he was overlooked in the White Sox front office; anyway, he was not among those permitted to continue throwing the spitter in the majors when the rule was enacted in 1919 for the 1920 season and thereafter. So he went back to the Pacific Coast League, where he could throw it without subterfuge and where, from 1920 to 1938, he won 296 games with its help.

Although a good deal of indignation has been expressed about the unfairness of depriving him of a legal means of livelihood in the majors, none of it came from Frank himself. "I am not bitter about it," he said in 1955 when he was back in the majors as pitching coach for the New York Giants. "I enjoyed my playing years and life in California. I have no regrets. I do have six children and 24 grandchildren. I'm fifty-eight and feel wonderful."

Shellenback, describing the spitter as "the perfect pitch for the man with a good fastball and no curve," said he got his first instruction in its use from Ed Walsh, who as a major league pitcher from 1904 to 1917 won 195 games in which his strikeout to bases-on-balls ratio was nearly 3 to 1. Shellenback honed his sensitive use of it on the teachings of two White Sox teammates, Eddie Cicotte and Red Faber, both master helmsmen of its flight. As a coach, Shellenback was circumspect about any success he may have had teaching it, with an illegally tampered ball, to Giant pitchers, but Jim Brosnan, a clever pitcher and witty writer (*Pennant Race* and *The Long Season*), in 1966 described the Shellenback-taught Giants as "a club that annually leads the National League in denying that its pitchers throw spitballs."

Shellenback wet, gripped, and delivered the ball in much the same way as did Grimes and most other masters of its down-spinning break: "It is held like the fastball with the two fingers on top of the ball wet. Naturally, the slippery top moves out first, and the ball spins with a forward motion—unlike the fastball, where the spin is counterclockwise. The wrist is not involved. It need not necessarily be stiff. It just follows natural action with no twist. The spitter spins and curves but demands less strain on the arm than any dry curve. The slippery part of the ball takes the place of violent wrist and arm twist."

How about a rainy day, when every ball gets wet? Is every pitch a spitter? Not so; quite the contrary, said Bill Doak, one of the last seventeen legal spitballers. The spitter requires one wet surface upon an otherwise dry ball, as a story he told illustrates:

"Once when I was pitching for the Cardinals with Branch Rickey managing, a light rain started to fall as I went out to hold a two-run lead in the fifth. I advised Rickey he had better warm up a pitcher in a hurry. 'Why?' he said. 'You're doing fine. Stay in there.' Well, in no time I blew that lead and we lost the game. Rickey asked me if I had had a premonition of disaster. 'No, Mr. Rickey,' I told him, 'when it rains and that ball is wet all over, a spitball pitcher just doesn't have any spitball.' "

There are those who have thrown the spitter as a spinless pitch behaving much like a knuckler. They achieve this effect by releasing the grip of thumb and bottom fingers when the top fingers slip away, "and the ball floats up like a knuckleball," as Eddie Lopat, the canny Yankee master of an assortment of weird junk pitches, described his. Joe Garagiola, veteran catcher turned raconteur and broadcaster, said he caught pitchers who threw wet knuckleballs. "They wet it and throw it like a knuckler, and they've got a knuckle spitter." The double effect of a spinless ball, reacting to air resistance on its undulating seams and to the "shine" lack of resistance on its wet surface, makes the ball's flight so erratically unpredictable that it is not much used; either effect is more than sufficient unto itself.

When thrown with great velocity, the shine side up, the spitter can become a wildly sailing fastball, dangerous to batters dug in for a sinker. Not out of regard for batters, but because of its unpredictability—it might sail up for a wild pitch or, again, its shine effect depressed by such variables as a following wind, come right down the middle into the batter's power—it is used only sparingly, mostly to add to the batter's anxiety.

It can be thrown with so many subtle variations, and its behavior is so subject to variable air conditions, that there is no universal agreement, among pitchers, batters, or umpires, on how it is thrown or what it will do. The uncertainty of batters facing a known spitballer is almost as important, perhaps equally as important, as the action of the next pitch. Set to hit its sinker effect, batters are frequently outwitted by a sneak fastball thrown up in the strike zone. Pitching it legally, Burleigh Grimes always concealed his mouth and fingers behind his glove, regardless of what pitch he was going to throw. Lew Burdette, a famous fidgeter, put it this way: "The spitter is my best pitch, and I don't throw it." A thinking batter is a pitcher's best friend, or, as Yogi Berra put it, "You can't hit and think at the same time."

Since 1949, there have been sporadic efforts, led and supported by top officials and esteemed veteran players, to repeal the prohibition of the spitter. Ford Frick, as National League president, was first to go out front in the efforts to make an honest pitch of the bootleg spitter. An Indianan of sturdy Bible Belt upbringing and a graduate of no-frills De Pauw University, Frick in his early wanderings was variously a semipro ballplayer, a college professor of English, a sports writer and general journalist, a ghost writer (for Babe Ruth), and a publicist for the National League. All this led, in 1935, at the age of forty-one, to the presidency of the league. From 1951 until 1965 he was Commissioner of Baseball. A firm administrator, he was respected for his persuasive ability to get owners and general managers to settle their squabbles and to calm the tensions of their differences in private discussions before they erupted into public confrontations. His personal integrity and his dedication to the integrity of the game were saluted upon his election to the Hall of Fame in 1970, eight years before his death.

Both personally and professionally, as a guardian of the reputation of the game, Frick was bothered at having on the books a rule that could not be fairly and effectively enforced and that was derisively being violated by a pitcher or two on every roster in both major leagues. His concerns are reflective of the way a host of fans, a legion of parents of young hero-worshippers, and some players think about professional (and much amateur) baseball's paradoxical ethics in accepting cheating on its own rules as a fundamental part of an otherwise incorruptible competition. Anything goes as long as you do it to win and don't get caught at it, etc.

There was nothing about the spitball that Ford Frick did not know and consider. He read the reports and cross-examined witnesses to flagrant violations. Affably, browsing around the baseball meetings, formal and informal, he got the views on the bootleg spitball, often while enjoying a taste of honest scotch, of owners, managers, coaches, players, umpires, and veterans. (He told me, I interject, about the complexity of his concerns, when he was baseball's commissioner, and I played a small, unpaid part as an advisor in his putting together a more systematic public relations program to enhance the reputation and widen the popularity of the game.)

Among others, Frick talked with tough Cal Hubbard, the American League umpire who in 1944 made the first (of only two) ejections of pitchers for throwing the spitball. Hubbard (whose professional career as a player was in football—the New York Giants and Green Bay Packers—and who is a member of both football's and baseball's halls of fame) told him that he ejected Nelson Potter of the Browns more because of his cantankerous defiance of Hubbard's warning to quit "huffing" on the ball than because of any proof he had that Potter was actually throwing spitballs. Hubbard and other umpires told Frick that a big difficulty of detection was that pitchers would fake "going to their mouths" both to invite inspection of an umblemished ball and to divert attention from other fidgets that got their fingers in contact with other concealments of clear and slippery goo. Hubbard was one of many umpires in favor of legalization. Frankie Frisch, then manager of the Chicago Cubs and no great reliever of the burdens that umpires bear, told Frick that if umpires called for and examined the ball after every suspected pitch, it would take up to five hours to play a game.

Toleration of cheating was as unacceptable to Frick as, he realized, a sanctimonious call from the front office for strict enforcement would be futile. So at the league meetings in December of 1949, knowing he would "get a lot of kidding," he suggested, rather mildly, that both leagues consider removing the spitball from 8.02. His own league did not even take a vote on it. Branch Rickey, president and general manager of the Brooklyn Dodgers, called the spitball "an unsanitary curiosity" and continued: "Give the pitchers the right to apply saliva to the ball and you might give them the impression that they would be winked at if they again laved the ball with tobacco juice, annointed it with oils, powdered it with talcum, or even stuck phonograph needles in it. It may be," he said with a philosophical sigh, "that the spitball would have survived if it had not been thrown into the company of all those trick deliveries."

At the American League meeting, Billy Evans, a former umpire and then general manager of the Detroit Tigers, approached Rickey's rhetorical splendor in arguing for rather than against legalization: "Heed the cries of the hurlers in their desert of dire need by letting them use the spitter." But the others, respectful of the drawing power of their home run hitters, were unswayed. In the vote that followed, only Evans voted aye.

Knocked out of that box, Frick made no further effort until he was securely established in his chair as Commissioner of Baseball, for which he was the popular choice in 1951 following the retirement, under fire, of A. B. (Happy) Chandler. In 1955 he risked the predictable disapproval of his employers and the inevitable storms of controversy, both inside and outside the leaky house of baseball, by again advocating the legalization of the spitter. In March of that year *The Sporting News* went to the sixteen spring training camps and asked 120 established players, managers, and coaches for their views on the commissioner's audacious proposal. The responses showed a big majority of sixty-four thinking right along with Frick, while thirty-six were opposed and twenty were on the fence.

To the wonderment of all, ten of the sixteen managers favored legalization. In speaking for many, Casey Stengel of the New York Yankees said it this way: "It's high time something was done for the pitchers. They put up stands and take down fences to make more home runs and plague the pitchers. Let them revive the spitter and help the pitchers make a living." Fred Haney of the Braves, who was in favor of retaining the ban, disagreed: "The pitchers don't need any more help, and the batting averages prove it. There is seldom a .350 hitter any more, and there hasn't been a .400 hitter for quite some time." Birdie Tebbetts of the Reds, who, with Walt Alston of the Dodgers, straddled the fence, declared that "it's immaterial to me, but I see no reason to revive it. All of us in baseball know that it's being thrown occasionally anyway."

Most pitchers and their coaches were with Frick. Ellis Kinder of the Red Sox: "Bring it back. I've got a dandy one already." Mike Garcia of the Indians: "I can really make it do tricks." But Bobby Shantz of the Athletics: "To satisfy the pitchers, let 'em shorten the bats and widen the plate." Most coaches agreed with Jim Turner of the Yankees: "It's not hard to throw, not difficult to teach and is easy on the arm. It sinks and makes a fine mixer with the high, hard one."

Being defensive players, infielders and outfielders were mainly opposed to the proliferation of its use that they thought legalization would bring. They envisioned its use as resulting in more errant throws because of the lingering "shine" on fielded spitballs. As batters, however, they were not of one mind. Al Rosen of the Indians: "Make it legal and I'll be able to hit .370 like the old-timers did." Gus Zernial of the Royals: "The pitchers can't control it and when they get behind in the count, they'll have to throw me the fast one. Baby, that's the one for me." Pee Wee Reese of the Dodgers: "I don't think legalizing the spitter would make such difference. They never stopped throwing it anyway." And, negatively, Jackie Jensen of the Red Sox: "Haven't they got enough pitches already? They might as well take our bats away."

But it was Frank Lane, then general manager of the Chicago White Sox, who summed up baseball's adamant rejection, then and later, of a legal spitter:

"It would be a return to the dead ball days. The Babe Ruth era was the beginning of baseball's tremendous growth in popularity. Power hitting and scoring are what the fans love to see. The spitter would bring back low-scoring games and cobwebs would start forming around the turnstiles.

"Besides, the spitter is a foul and unsanitary pitch. When some of the old spitball pitchers loaded the ball with saliva and slippery elm, it would be splattering all over the place. It can be seen from the stands, and the feminine clientele we have developed would find it objectionable."

Even so, Frick persisted in urging legalization, but rule 8.02 was still on the books when he retired as commissioner in 1965.

Joseph Cronin, following his brilliant career as power-hitting infielder of the Washington Senators and Boston Red Sox, was already in the game's Hall of Fame when, in 1959, he was elected president of the American League and took the lead in pushing for legalization of the spitter. Like Frick, and like all the others who have revived the appeal in more recent years, he gave it his best shot and fell back. Aside from fiddling and faddling with various rule changes to make the ban more enforceable, none of which got the job done, baseball management still echoes the rhetoric of Branch Rickey and Frank Lane.

While Frick and Cronin tried to get baseball out of cheating on the rule by getting rid of the rule, the owners preferred to deny that cheating exists to any considerable extent. When Birdie Tebbetts, a veteran catcher then managing the Cincinnati Reds, protested to Warren Giles, president of the National League, that the umpires had refused to enforce the rule in a game with the Milwaukee Braves in which Lew Burdette, whom Birdie described as "a dirty, cheating spitballer," was making flagrant use of his wet one, Giles looked into the spitter dilemma and, clearing the umpires and Lew, reported that "no National League pitcher is throwing it." Birdie's protest got nowhere, but neither did Burdette's demand that Birdie apologize for his unproved allegations.

But even Birdie was true to the player code whereby it is taboo to admit that a teammate throws it. After the Burdette affair, Frankie Frisch pressed him in a television interview to admit that, while catching for Tommy Bridges of the Detroit Tigers, it was a spitball he threw into the outfield in a 1941 game against the New York Yankees. Joe Gordon was at bat. Marse Joe McCarthy was sure that Tommy was throwing spitters. When a suspicious pitch zipped away from Tebbetts, Marse Joe hollered for Gordon to grab it for evidence. Both Gordon and Tebbetts pounced upon the ball. Tebbetts got it away from Gordon and heaved it into the outfield. By the time it came back, having been handled three times en route, umpire Bill McGowan found it to be dry.

"Bridges must have done something to that ball," Frankie persisted.

"Let's put it this way," Birdie replied, enjoying the recollection, "It was exciting while it lasted."

Joe DiMaggio had the code in mind even in retirement, when he was asked if Johnny Allen of the Indians was a spitballer. "I can't be positive," he said. "I sometimes missed that sinker of his day by a foot. It wasn't a curve and it wasn't a fastball, so I took it for granted it was a slider. But come to think about it," he added, thinking about it, "I did not in those days miss sliders by a foot."

Because no working pitcher can afford to help umpires identify his use of it by admitting that he does throw it, and because the ejection penalty for getting caught using it has been inflicted only twice since 1920, there can be no reliable count, now or ever, of consistent and occasional spitballers. The prevalent, but privately expressed, opinion of insiders is that there is at least one habitual offender on every roster and that there are, now and usually, about fifty of the two hundred or so pitchers on major league rosters who throw it (or the scuffball) often enough to merit a mention at team briefings before opposing teams go forth to face them. Far from following their perfunctory denials with slander or libel action, most suspected spitballers and scuffballers enjoy their reputations, and find it helpful in fooling batters.

After retirement, the denials tend to diminish. Some, like Preacher Roe of the Dodgers who wrote a book about "me'n the spitter," enjoy the fame and admiration it brought to them. Others—such as Schoolboy Rowe, Whitey (aka Slick) Ford, Sal Maglie, George (Red) Munger, Joe Page, Don Drysdale, Bob Turley, among the host—either do not deny having used it, or else are jocularly evasive when questioned. No shame, in any case, is on them, nor is their adulation by the fans akin to that for the outlaws Frank and Jesse James, or of legendary Robin Hood. The successful spitballers are admired as diligent craftsmen who always did their best to get the batters out, to help their teams win, and to prolong their employment in the game they love.

All of which brings us to Gaylord Perry who, in his final major league season in 1983, at forty-four was the oldest player in the majors and in his twenty-third year of employment as a big league pitcher. He had by this time moved into third place, ahead of Walter Johnson's 3,508, in career strikeouts. He had won 307 games—more than any contemporary—for the seven clubs he worked for—and in 1983 won seven more for the Mariners and Kansas City Royals to bring his win total to 314. Twice winner of the Cy Young Award, he seems a shoo-in for the Hall of Fame in the first year of his eligibility.

In addition to his artful dissembling on the mount, Perry's pitching success is indebted to the genes and the boyhood training he received in his birthplace, Williamston, North Carolina. His older brother, James Evans Perry, Jr., preceded him as a distinguished major league pitcher. Jim, also a Cy Young award winner in 1970, won 215 games for the Indians, Twins, and Tigers in his seventeen years in the majors, retiring at thirty-eight in 1975. Gaylord does not credit Jim with teaching him the spitter, because he does not admit to throwing it, but the genetic inheritance is obvious; both are big, strong, tough, talented, and competitive athletes.

On Monday, August 23, 1982, Gaylord Perry, pitching in Seattle against the Boston Red Sox, became the second pitcher in the sixty-two-year history of rule 8.02 to be ejected, suspended, and fined for throwing a spitter. The umpire was Dave Phillips, generally respected—but not by Gaylord—for his twelve years of calling them as he saw them in the American League. After observing several pitches sink with more magic than he thought good spin could put on them, he stopped the game, still scoreless, in the fifth and went to the mound and asked to see the ball.

"It looked to me like there was some slick substance on it," he said, telling about it.

"What kind?" asked Dennis Dillon, sportswriter for the St. Louis *Globe-Democrat*.

"I am an umpire, not a chemist. After I warned him, he said something to the effect that 'you ain't seen nothin' yet.' I wasn't sure if he meant I hadn't found anything or if he meant he had something else in store."

In the seventh, the Red Sox scored the first run of the game and had runners at first and third, two out, and a two-ball, no-strike count on Rick Miller.

"The next pitch was a classic example of an illegal pitch," Phillips said. "It came in like a fastball and the bottom dropped out." He called it a strike, but "I didn't hesitate. I called time and went out and raised my arm that he was ejected. You can warn or eject on the flight of the ball, and that's what I did," he told reporters. "Then I went out and got the ball and it felt like there was a slippery substance on it."

He sent the ball to the league headquarters as evidence to support the ejection, and Lee McPhail, league president suspended Perry for ten days and fined him $250.

Gaylord was indignant. He called McPhail a "weak human" for upholding Phillips's call and said that "Phillips seems to have it in for us. No other umpire is as bad as Dave Phillips." He said the pitch he threw to Miller behaved no differently than "a forkball thrown by Bruce Sutter." But Phillips's last words on the subject prevailed: "Gaylord Perry has a history of this stuff. He was in a tough situation with men on first and third, and in my mind he threw an illegal pitch. He did what he did, and I did what I have to do."

The game went on, and what happened is illustrative of how the ejection on suspicion of a star pitcher can be, and frequently is, a determinant in victory or defeat, and why it is so rarely called. Phillips changed his strike call to a ball on that pitch to Miller. As replacement for Perry, Ed VandeBerg came to the mound with a two-ball, no-strike count. He walked Miller to load the bases. Mike Stanton, relieving, then walked Dwight Evans, giving the Red Sox a 2–0 lead, and they went on to win the game by 4–3.

The spitter, one can conclude, is here to stay.

Generally recognized as one of baseball's top pitching coaches, Hub Kittle shows young Andy Rincon how he should be grasping the ball at the halfway point in his release. *The Sporting News*

The 100+ MPH fastball of Nolan Ryan, en route to the plate. *The Sporting News*

The fingers of his pitching hand still spread from delivering his split-fingered fastball, Bruce Sutter follows through in classic fashion. *The Sporting News*

CHAPTER FIFTEEN

The No-Hitters that the Curve Makes Possible

I played golf alone that day, thinking more about how to get into this chapter, for which I had a floor full of scattered notes, than about hitting the golf ball. I smiled when the thought occurred that this ball wasn't coming at me with a curveball's deception or a fastball's zip, but was just sitting there in the sand trap waiting to be hit. I noticed that it was smiling back at me—not so much a smile as a crooked grin, put there, no doubt, by the 9-iron that had punched it into the trap instead of pitching it onto the green. I played lousy golf. I couldn't figure out how to get this chapter started without using dry statistics to support my premise that all of the 196 no-hitters pitched since 1875— with how many? perhaps five exceptions—had been achieved with curveball-fastball mixes that kept batters from timing their swings precisely enough to get even a single base hit.

This was at the South Fork Country Club in the village of Amaganset in the town of East Hampton in the county of Suffolk in the state of New York on July 4, 1983, the 207th birthday of the United States of America, "when in the course of human events . . ."

There were only four guys at the bar of our modest clubhouse, drinking beers and checking their cards to figure out how many two-bit wagers each had coming from—and owed to—whom. Casual attention was being paid to the television images, without sound, coming from Yankee Stadium, where the Boston Red Sox were visitors. Curt Becker, the only real baseball fan in the foursome, included me in the round of beers he owed for most tee shots sliced into the rough, and remarked that Dave Righetti, the Yankee's young lefthander, had a no-hitter going after five innings. "And he's doing it with fastballs."

"Well," I said, confident of my statistics, "it would be a miracle if he pitched a no-hitter using only fastballs. It's almost never been done. Walter Johnson did it twice, but one of his was called after seven because of darkness."

"How about Feller? He pitched three of them."

"But only the first—the one he pitched in the opening game of the 1940 season—was with pure smoke. He had a good curve working for him in his other two."

"And Nolan Ryan with his five?"

"Same thing. Maybe his first . . ." Young David was now pitching in the sixth, and Curt and I were paying close attention to every pitch, especially those we could follow from the view of the center-field camera. "Looky there! The kid's got a heck of a sinker."

"Yes, yes!" said Curt. "looks like a sinking slider."

"And a change-up curve."

Even with his good mix, the odds against Righetti pitching a no-hitter were very great. I got to thinking about the strangest one of all, when Hoyt Wilhelm fashioned his no-hitter on September 20, 1958, in a 1–0 win over the Yankees with nothing but curves—mainly the knuckler variety. As a measure of how much good pitching, good fielding, good luck, and everything else—including good air and wind conditions—it takes to achieve a no-hitter, Hoyt was the first Baltimore Oriole to pitch one since James Hughes of the old Orioles did it in 1898. (To be sure, from 1903 until 1953 the Orioles were out of the majors. But even so . . .)

In his no-hitter Hoyt threw 99 pitches, of which 87 were knucklers and the other 12 were also curves, mostly sinkers. Without throwing a single fastball, he struck out eight batters, including Elston Howard and Hank Bauer twice each, retired fourteen on pop-ups and flyballs, and got six on grounders. (Of the twenty-eight batters he faced, he walked two, but one was cut down trying to steal second.)

How did he do it?

Well, he said in his easy Carolinian drawl, he had such good control of his knuckler that he was able to change speeds on it, "something I often can't do." Part of the reason for that, he went on, was that the weather, though drizzly from the second inning on, was favorable because the slight winds were never from behind. "It's when you get a wind blowing in behind you that you fear. A knuckler seldom does anything then, because it's a nonrotation pitch that does better against air resistance." The way it was, he said, "my knuckler was behaving mighty well for me. A lot of pitches were sort of half speed and others I gave a little more snap." Then he added the indispensable ingredient of every no-hitter: "It takes a good bit of luck to pitch a no-hitter, regardless of the stuff a fellow may have."

When did he begin thinking no-hitter? "Not seriously" until Gus Triandos hit the 425-foot homer into dead center in the seventh inning against Bobby Shantz that gave the Orioles a 1–0 lead. "You've got to get at least one run to win. There's nothing that peps a pitcher up like scoring. After that, I began to think I could get them all out. Finally, I began to figure it out myself—six more to go, then five and finally, when Bauer came up, one more left."

Hank Bauer, as tough an honest competitor as the game has known, but not a good curveball hitter, decided to take advantage of Wilhelm's slowness afoot, especially on the wet grass. Hank dropped a bunt that would have been a sure hit had it not just barely rolled foul. Then Bauer, swinging hard at a knuckler, popped a fly into short right-center, and Hoyt's curveball no-hitter was baseball history. It was, by the way, the fifth no-hitter pitched on a September 20th, going back to 1882—the most for any one day of the year.

Contemplating Dave Righetti's slim chance to register the third no-hitter pitched on a Fourth of July, I tried to remember how long it had been since Nolan Ryan had pitched the last hitless game (his fifth!) in the major leagues, but the date eluded me, as it did Curt. (It was nearly two years before—on September 26, 1981, a 5–0 Houston win over Los Angeles.)

The line score on the screen after the Red Sox went down in the sixth showed the Yankees ahead 2–0, with 0 runs, 0 hits, and 0 errors for the visitors.

"Turn up the sound!" someone yelled.

"No sound!" quoth Curt. "I don't want to hear any idiot announcer jinx the kid by even mentioning no-hitter. And that," he added out of stern respect for the ancient baseball tradition that forbids mention of a no-hitter from the seventh inning on, "goes for us, too. I don't want to be a party to any jinx."

And so, while the Red Sox were batting, we opened our mouths only to admit the cold stuff. And somehow, as it does on the diamond, respect for the tradition added to the tension as the slim possibility grew to a reasonable chance and rose, fragile as a soap bubble in the winds of fortune, toward an almost impossible attainment.

From our vantage point behind the young man—as handsomely courageous as any hero of myth or legend "facing fearful odds/for the glory of his fathers and the temples of his gods"—we watched his power pitches sail up and away from the righthanded batters, and up and in to the lefties at the plate. Mixing these fast balls with sinking curves (mostly quick sliders, as best we could judge), young David kept the determined Boston challengers off balance and off base through the seventh inning.

In their eighth, the Yankees remained at bat a long, long twenty minutes, scoring two more runs. Thinking of David in the dugout, I kept hoping the Yankees would go down quickly, before his mind and muscles tightened. The two new runs, while practically assuring victory, seemed irrelevant to the no-hitter. Or—second and third thoughts—were they? Would they give him more confidence in teasing the corners, without concern that a walk or sudden home run could turn the game around? Or would they give him a sense of security that would seduce him into taking something off the action of his pitches in order to make sure he was throwing strikes?

My worries were not his. He went out to the mound calm and loose. "I was just going to let it all hang out," he said after the game. "I wanted to keep their guys off base before the big guys like Jim Rice and Tony Armas got a chance."

But his sailing fastballs and sinking curves missed their mark, and he walked Jeff Newman to start the ninth. Oh, no! Oh, no! Like a lone raven over arrayed troops before battle, a lead-off walk is a baseball omen of disaster. Young David, however, did not see it that way.

"I knew that he (Glen Hoffman, standing in) would be trying to go to leftfield with the ball, like he did two years ago when he broke up a no-hitter I had going in the seventh, so I kept it down and in on him and hoped we'd get a grounder."

He did, and got a double-play grounder—to second base for one, and over to first for . . . but, no, the stretch to catch the throw took the first baseman's foot an inch or two off the bag as Hoffman crossed it safely. One still on and two outs to go, with the top of the Red Sox order coming up. The Yankee infielders came toward the mound. "I told them to relax, you'll get another grounder." This one was a bounder to second baseman Andre Robertson, easy to field but slow getting to him. A quick glance showed he had little chance to force the running, sliding Hoffman at second, so Robertson threw to first for the more certain out, retiring Jerry Remy, the batter. Man on second, one out to go.

Now only Wade Boggs stood between Dave and the no-hitter. With a .361 batting average at the time, Wade was the most productive batter in the Red Sox lineup (and in either league, for that matter). Lefthander against lefthanded batter gave Righetti a slight percentage edge. "If I'm going to lose it then, it's going to be off my best stuff, hard fastballs, then a slider." Four fastballs took the scoreboard lights to deuces wild—2 balls, 2 strikes, 2 outs. Boggs had no better option than to get set to pull the trigger on another fastball in the strike zone. His swing was over and ahead of the sinking slider. Young David got the final strike of his no-hitter with a curveball.

Thus it was that Dave Righetti pitched the 197th major league no-hitter since Joe Borden of Philadelphia held the Chicago Cubs hitless one hundred and eight years earlier, on July 28, 1875.

In reviewing Dave's chances of pitching another hitless game in his next start, Phil Pepe of the New York *Daily News* calculated that the odds against pitching a no-hitter on any given start in the major leagues are about 1,200 to 1. On this basis, several of his readers calculated, the odds against pitching two consecutive no-hitters are 1,400,000 to 1. Would anybody care to calculate what the odds would be against pitching two in a row without using curves?

Dave set down the first three batters he faced in his next start, against Kansas City on July 9, but Hal McRae tripled to open the second inning, ending Righetti's string of no-hit innings at ten.

There were two other no-hit games during the 1983 season, in addition to Righetti's. One of them, for the Oakland A's against the

Chicago White Sox at Oakland on September 29, was hurled by a twenty-two-year-old rookie, Mike Warren, who had begun the season in Class A ball with Albany in the Eastern League. Warren walked three batters, but one of them was thrown out attempting to steal second, so the Oakland rookie faced only twenty-nine batters. The other hitless masterpiece was created by the St. Louis Cardinals' Bob Forsch, against Montreal in a night game at Busch Stadium September 26. It was Forsch's second no-hit performance, the first having come in 1978.

Vern Rapp, the Expos' first base coach, had been manager of the Cardinals when Forsch had thrown his first no-hitter. "That time," he recalled, "Bob got it with only a fastball and a slider. This time he mixed them with the good change-up he has developed." The first no-hitter was somewhat tainted in the minds of some of the fans and all of the Philadelphia Phillies because Gary Maddox's hard shot to Ken Reitz at third base might just as easily have been ruled too-hot-to-handle instead of an error on Reitz. The 1983 masterpiece, however, was all but flawless; Forsch gave up one base on balls, and another runner reached first when the Cardinals' second baseman, Ken Oberkfell, let Chris Speier's grounder scoot between his legs for an unquestioned error. Otherwise the bases were kept empty of Expos throughout the contest. Forsch became the twenty-fifth major league pitcher to rack up more than one no-hit game. He is planning, he says, to develop a knuckleball to add to his repertory in future years.

Only Johnny Vander Meer has ever thrown consecutive no-hit major league baseball games. Pitching for the Cincinnati Reds at home on June 11, 1938, he held the Boston Braves hitless in a 3–0 victory. Then, in his next start, on June 15 in Brooklyn, he pitched another no-hitter against the Dodgers in a 6–0 win. Against the odds of something like 172,800,000 to 1 against anybody pitching three in a row he started against the Braves in Boston on June 19. He pitched two more hitless innings before giving up a hit to Debs Garms in the third. The twenty hitless innings he pitched in those three games is the National League record for consecutive hitless innings by a starting pitcher. Cy Young holds the major league record of twenty-four consecutive hitless innings. His streak included innings he pitched in games before and after his perfect (when nobody reaches base in any manner) no-hitter of May 5, 1905, for the Boston Red Sox against the Philadelphia Athletics, winning 3–0. Cy, of course, pitched two other no-hitters—one for the Cleveland Indians in 1897 and the other for the Red Sox in 1908.

Ewell Blackwell came closest of any other pitcher to pitching two consecutive no-hitters. On June 18, 1947, at home in Cincinnati, he pitched one against the Boston Braves in a 6–0 win. Next time out, against the Brooklyn Dodgers in Ebbets Field, he went to the mound in the ninth inning with a no-hitter going. He got the lead-off man, but then Eddie Stanky singled and so did Jackie Robinson, the next batter up, to make it just another good try and no cigar.

While setting the American League record of three no-hitters and tying with Cy Young (one of whose was in the National League) for three in the majors, Bob Feller came closer than any pitcher, including Nolan Ryan, to putting the record for most no-hitters out of sight. Before his first no-hitter on opening day of the 1940 season, he had pitched three one-hitters. While he may have experimented with a few curves, it seems fair to give his fastball all the credit for his first no-hitter and those three close encounters. Before his second no-hitter, accomplished with a curve to mix into his repertory, against the Yankees at New York on April 30, 1946, he had pitched three more one-hit games. Prior to his third, the opener of a doubleheader against the Detroit Tigers on July 1, 1951, he had pitched four one-hitters and went on to pitch two more, for a lifetime total of twelve one-hitters and three no-hitters.

In a duel with Bob Cain of the St. Louis Browns on April 23, 1952, Feller lost a one-hitter on a lead-off triple by Bobby Young in the first inning, followed by an error, to make the score 1–0. Cain's shutout was also a one-hitter, so between them they set the record in the American League for fewest hits by both teams in one game.

Nolan Ryan, meanwhile, has pitched eight one-hitters to go with his all-time record of five hitless games, perhaps only the first of which was achieved without strong reliance on change-up curves to set up his 100-MPH plus fastball.

First to break the record of three no-hitters was Sandy Koufax, whose curve was said to emit an audible sizzle. His record-breaking fourth no-hit game, a 1–0 win over the Chicago Cubs for the Los Angeles Dodgers on September 9, 1965, was only the tenth perfect game since 1880, when John Richmond of Worcester threw one against Cleveland. Since then Jim (Catfish) Hunter, with Oakland against the Minnesota Twins on May 8, 1968, and Len Barker, with Cleveland against the Toronto Blue Jays on May 15, 1981, have also pitched no-hitters of nine or more innings in which nobody got on base.

The strangest perfect no-hit game, one in which Babe Ruth was the starting pitcher, was that by Ernie Shore of the Boston Red Sox vs. the Washington Senators on June 23, 1917. Ruth, the Red Sox starter, pitching to Ray Morgan, the first batter, got so upset with the balls Brick Owens called that after walking Morgan, he strode in to let the umpire know verbally and, some say, by taking a poke at him, what he thought of his ball-and-strike judgment. Brick ordered Ruth out of the game. Shore came to the mound and, without warming up, pitched to the second batter. Morgan was thrown out trying to steal second. and Shore went on to get the next twenty-six batters out. Since all twenty-seven were retired while he was on the mound, there is strong justification for designating it a perfect game.

If the Babe had not been such a prodigious hitter of curveballs—and fastballs, too, of course—he might well have gone into the Hall of Fame as a pitcher. After part of a year in the minors, Ruth came up to the Boston Red Sox in 1914 as a nineteen-year-old lefthanded pitcher with a curve so mean it was called a "hook" and with a buzzing fastball that started to sink, then leveled off in the strike zone.

While he never pitched a no-hitter, he would undoubtedly have notched a few had he remained a pitcher instead of becoming a good outfielder and the mightiest batter in all of baseball. As it was, he pitched 163 major league games, all but five for the Red Sox in the 1914–19 period, winning 94 and losing 46 with a 2.28 earned-run average. In the second game of the 1916 World Series, he gave up a home run in the first inning, then pitched thirteen scoreless innings to beat the Dodgers, 2–1, when Del Gainor doubled home the winning run in the gloaming of the fourteenth inning. He continued his scoreless inning streak in World Series competition by shutting out the Chicago Cubs, 1–0, in the first game in 1918 and by pitching seven more runless innings in the fourth game, for a total of twenty-three and two-thirds scoreless World Series innings, a record that stood until Whitey Ford exceeded it in 1961 with a total of thirty-three. The Babe's earned-run average for the three World Series games he won for the Red Sox (as against no losses) was 0.87. Whitey Ford, who pitched in 498 games for the New York Yankees, winning 236, never got the proverbial cigar for pitching a no-hitter, either.

Of the 199 major league no-hitters—the most fortuitous may well have been the second of two no-hitters that Allie (The Chief) Reynolds pitched for the Yankees in 1951. The first was a 1–0 thriller over Bob Feller and the Cleveland Indians on July 12. On September 28, he had a no-hitter going with two out in the ninth and only Ted

Williams of the Boston Red Sox to get out. Ted got under a hard slider and fouled it high and back. Yogi Berra circled and waited under it—and dropped it for an error. The Chief bore down on Ted with another slider. Again Ted fouled it into the heavens. This time Yogi made the catch. Was Reynolds upset when Berra dropped the first one? "No," he said at the Old-Timers game before the 1983 All-Star game, "I wasn't. That's part of the game, but—" he went on, shaking his head, "if Williams had got a hit, Yogi never would have forgiven himself."

There is no reliable way to count the no-hitters that have been achieved without curves. Give Walter Johnson both of his, one in seven innings. Give Feller and Nolan one each. And, more surely, give Paul Dean one for the 3–0 no-hitter he pitched for the St. Louis Cardinals over the Brooklyn Dodgers in the second game of a doubleheader on September 21, 1934. Brother Dizzy, who had won a three-hit, 13–0 slaughter in the first game, got after Paul for not telling him he was going to fire a no-hitter in the second game. "You shoulda tole Ol' Diz you was gonna do it, and I'da gone out there an' done it, too." Dizzy never won that no-hitter cigar either.

Beginning in October of 1903, when the Boston Red Sox and Pittsburgh Pirates played in the first World Series (best of nine, which the Sox won in eight games), there had never been a no-hitter pitched in the fifty-three world championship classics. On October 8, 1956, it was achieved by a pitcher who, off his previous pitching record, would have been a leader only if a vote had been taken to determine pitchers least likely to pitch one. It was Don Larsen who did it—not only did it but pitched a perfect game, twenty-seven up and twenty-seven down, the only one of its kind in World Series history. The curveball was the key.

Don was a big handsome guy, a natty dresser, better known for spending money after hours than earning it on the mound. He had come to Casey Stengel and the New York Yankees in 1954 as a spear-carrier in a big trade with Baltimore, where he had won 3 and lost 21 games. In spring training at St. Petersburg the next March, Don, out after curfew, drove his car into a power pole, snapping it and wrecking the car, but got back to training camp uninjured. Instead of fining him, Casey gave him a fatherly lecture and shipped him to Denver, then in the American Association. Don worked hard there and had a 9–1 record when Casey called him back to finish the season with the Yankees, winning 9 and losing 2. But he became one of the goats in the 1955 World Series, which the Yankees lost to the Brooklyn Dodgers, by getting clobbered in four innings of the fourth game, when the Dodgers evened the Series at two games each.

In the 1956 season, Don pitched reliably, winning 11 and losing 5 of his 20 starts and 18 relief assignments as the Yankees again won the American League pennant and again squared off against the Dodgers in the World Series. The Dodgers won the first game, and Larsen, starting the second, got bombed out in the second inning as the Dodgers won again, 13–8. But the Yankees won the next two, so the Series was tied when Stengel called upon Larsen to try again.

He threw 97 pitches and set down the Dodgers 1–2–3 for nine innings. One of his seven strikeouts came in the first inning, after the only time he threw as many as three balls to any batter. With a 3–2 count, he got Pee Wee Reese on a called strike. Of course, as all no-hit pitchers must, he got fine support from his fielders.

As with most World Series crowds, the 64,519 spectators in Yankee Stadium were mostly just that—spectators, not the real fans who mostly are ignored when the privileges of buying World Series tickets are doled out. But by the seventh inning, the rare magnificence of Larsen's pitching had became apparent even to these strangers in paradise.

The possibility of seeing a perfect game pitched enthralled the crowd, but not the players, who were playing to protect or else to destroy the 2–0 Yankee lead. "I was after the game first and anything I could get after that," said Don. Yogi Berra, catching Don and calling the pitches, was fearful of a walk and a homer. Knowing the batters, he continued to call a mix of sinking curves, sliders, and fastballs, confident of Don's superb control of all of them that day. Carl Furillo, first up in the ninth, hit four fouls off curves and sliders before, on an 0–2 fastball, he flied out. Roy Campanella fouled the first sinker for a strike and grounded out on the next one.

Now Sal Maglie, who had pitched well enough to win almost any game, was due up at the plate. But Walter Alston, Dodger manager, called for Dale Mitchell, a lefthanded batter, to keep his club's chances alive. Dale took a curve outside for a ball, a slider for a called strike, swung at and missed a curve, fouled another low curve. With a one-ball and two-strike count, Yogi called for, and Don threw, a fastball that Dale thought was outside, but that umpire Babe Pinelli called strike three. "It was too close to take," said Babe, who was umpiring his last game of a twenty-two-year major league career, "and if I had to do it again, I'd still call it a strike."

Don attributed his perfect game to the no-windup delivery he had begun using only two weeks before. "I was giving something away [tell-tales] to the batters in my wind-up. They knew what was coming in. They were stealing my stuff, and I made up my mind to go with the no-windup delivery. Well, it has worked to perfection. I fool the batters better, and I have better control. It's wonderful."

There are those who believe that Don had Something Else working for him that day. Many in baseball, as in all types of risky human endeavor over the centuries, attribute much of what would be otherwise inexplicable good and evil experiences to the observance or neglect of traditional ritual, prayer, or placation. It is the participation of other than human forces that determines how this thing is going to turn out; call them what one will: God, the Fates, demons, or Lady Luck. It is a fact that the principal broadcasters of Don's perfect game, Vin Scully and Bob Wolff, alternating between radio and television, scrupulously avoided outright mention of the noun phrase "no-hitter." Vin put it this way: "Mr. Don Larsen through seven innings has retired twenty-one men in a row." Wolff was even less explicit: "I just can't describe all that is going on as far as Larsen is concerned, but I'm sure that all who are listening are well-informed."

After the game, Don's father, back home in Berkeley, California, said, "I got down on my knees and prayed for Don. No, I didn't pray for a no-hitter. I just asked God to help Don beat the Bums." Don's mother refused to watch the game because "every time I watch him, he loses."

On the way to the Stadium that day, Don told the cabbie: "I got a feeling I'm going to pitch a no-hitter."

"Did you pray for one?" the cabbie asked.

Don, a Lutheran, admitted he had not. "But here," he said, handing the cabbie a $5 bill, "give this to your synagogue."

Larsen's perfect game won him a big salary hike, which his entertainment proclivities required. He enjoyed a few decent pitching years after that, but never again came close to throwing a no-hitter, let alone a perfect game. He had won 81 and lost 91 in his fourteen-year major league career when he was cast adrift for the last time in 1967, by the Chicago Cubs.

Though the most historic performance in World Series history, Don Larsen's was neither the longest or the most remarkable example of perfect pitching in baseball's hundred-and-eight-year history of no-hitters. That was the work of Harvey Haddix, a curveball, change-up artist.

I was homeward bound on a dinky highway through the emerging corn and soybean fields of Central Illinois. It was lonely and lovely out there on the prairie, that night of May 26, 1959. I had been enjoying the broadcast of the Cardinal game, which went in and out of my consciousness without a trace of memory. Then the broadcast was switched to Milwaukee, where Harvey Haddix of the Pittsburgh Pirates had held the Braves hitless and off-base into the ninth inning of a 0–0 game.

Since Haddix was a hero of mine from his years as a St. Louis Cardinal, I was offended to hear the broadcasters put the jinx on him by using "no-hitter" and "perfect game" as they whooped up the drama of it. There are, as we have seen, other ways—"retired the last twenty-seven batters," "and at the end of nine, it's zero, zero, and zero for the Braves," etc.—to let a fan know the situation without inviting the wrath of the baseball divinities.

Oblivious of any curse the broadcasters might have been placing on his efforts, however, Harvey pitched on and on—through the tenth, eleventh . . . the twelfth—the longest perfect game in all of baseball history! He was doing it with curves and change-ups; they were all he had to offer, and quite all that he needed.

Leading off in the thirteenth, Felix Mantilla grounded—off what? those damn announcers weren't calling the kinds of pitches, either— a pitch to Don Hoak at third, and was safe at first on an error when Don's throw was not quite there. So the perfect game was gone; but the no-hitter was still alive. Ed Matthews bunted Mantilla to second and was out at first. Pirate strategy called for an intentional walk to Hank Aaron, so now runners were at first and second, with one out, and Joe Adcock advancing to the plate.

"Come on, Kitten!" I hollered to the corn and beans, "A double-play ground ball, and we're out of it!" (St Louis fans had called Harvey the Kitten when he was a teammate of Harry [the Cat] Brecheen.)

But the mighty Adcock smacked a double—or, possibly, a home run; the announcers did not seem to know which. Out of their confusion, anyway, the fact ultimately emerged that both Mantilla and Aaron had scored, and Harvey had lost, 2–0.

Officially, the next day, Warren Giles, National League president, ruled that Aaron, thinking it was a homer, had been overrun by Adcock, and so only Felix Mantilla's run counted. So it's in the books that Harvey Haddix, having pitched the longest perfect game in history, lost that game in the thirteenth inning, by the score of 1–0.

The announcers took the babble of the press box down to a weary
Haddix in a depressed Pirate clubhouse. The first guy to get to Harvey
stuck a microphone in his face and blurted: "Would you say, Harvey,
that this is the best game you ever pitched?"

I almost drove off the road.

Pete Vuckovich's Cy Young Award pitching performance for the Milwaukee Brewers in 1982 came to an end
when he ran out of gas in the sixth inning of the final game of the 1982 World Series. *Russ Reed*

Bob McClure, who came in to relieve for Milwaukee in the deciding game of the 1982 World Series, and, at right, his longtime friend Keith Hernandez, who is shown in the act of stroking the base hit that won the game and the series for the St. Louis Cardinals. *Gary Weber; St. Lous Globe-Democrat.*

CHAPTER SIXTEEN

Decisions, Decisions, Decisions— In Which Number Two Is Not Thrown to Keith Hernandez, and . . .

"**B**aseball is a dull game only to a dull mind." Fully to appreciate Red Barber's classic summation of the fascination of baseball for so many millions of us, imagine, the next time you are at the ballpark or in front of a television screen, that there are cartoon balloons—like the kind in the funny papers—arising from the heads of the batter and the nine defensive players. Each will be crowded with a gibberish of what-ifs, then-what's, and can-I's. You can only guess at what they are guessing and deciding and hoping. But you will observe that the balloons arising from the catcher's and batter's heads are twice as large as those over all the other players on the field—except the pitcher's, whose balloon is as large as all the others put together.

Or perhaps it would be easier, in these days of silicon chips, to imagine each player's mind as a computer, in which alternatives and anticipations and responses are incorporated in a data memory bank of baseball wisdom going back a hundred years, and being updated constantly with fresh data on what opponents did and are likely to do in any situation.

The pitcher has the most decisions to make, because he has the most alternatives. The batter has fewer, since he cannot make a decision until the pitcher has made his—in addition to which, some of his pre-pitch decisions are made for him by his bench. The infielders and outfielders are preprogrammed, through repetitive practice and training, to make the plays required by the game situation, about which they remind themselves and each other before the pitcher decides what he is going to do. But once the brain trust on the bench has made its basic decisions, based on a complexity of memories, it is as helpless to carry them out as any fan in the stands. All now depends upon the pitcher. The catcher suggests; the pitcher decides—though sometimes the managerial bench instructs both of them on what to do, Or Else.

Before determining what pitch to throw and where to try to throw it, the pitcher—depending upon his sensitivity, versatility, acquired wisdom, and respect for the catcher's opinion—may well make as many as fifty decisions, choices between alternatives, and then add a few more while in his delivery movements. A ball with high seams will give more action to his curveball assortment, but will take a foot of velocity off his fastball. If he is primarily a fastball pitcher, he may consider going with his curve—but then, the batter may be a better curveball than a fastball hitter, so perhaps his fastball is the better choice. Is the wind with him, against him, or coming from across the diamond? And how fast, and how consistently? Is the air unusually thin or thick? Is the ball in his hand on the light or heavy side of the quarter-ounce difference permitted in its manufacture? Does it have a slick grass stain or an accidental scuff on it? If not, is this the time to put one or the other on its surface?

The stadium he is pitching in brings up another complex of choices. If it is night, how good are the lights? If it is day, in whose favor are sunshine and shade? Why is this normally upright batter waiting there in a crouch? What is he expecting? If he's digging in for a sinker, how about a fastball up and in?

And what's riding on this pitch? The game? The season? A trip back to the buses in the minors?

But, with a five-run lead, what's the big deal? This might be a good time to try out the knuckler he's been throwing in the bullpen.

The master pitcher is certainly not conscious of all the considerations that go into his final decision. Out of his experience, competitiveness, and confidence, he trusts the decision that his computer-like mind makes. He concentrates on the mechanics of throwing that pitch to the desired spot. His intense competitiveness is tempered by the knowledge that you can't win 'em all, that some of 'em are gonna be basehits, that luck and the call of the umpire may be with or against you. Awareness that "it ain't all up to me" reduces the fear of failing that would otherwise increase the possibility of failure, and adds to his confidence. The thought that "maybe he'll hit it at somebody" makes it all the more likely that the batter won't hit it at all.

The less experienced, less skilled pitcher—say a rookie, much in awe of these major league heroes he is now facing—is much too conscious of the alternatives he confronts in making a pitching decision, and too fearful of the consequences. He is throwing with desperate hope instead of with ingrained confidence. His mind is like a malfunctioning computer, short-circuited by too much conscious thought. The bad things he is afraid will happen start to happen. He can't pitch as well as he is capable of pitching.

Often, however, in the you-against-me, pitcher-batter confrontations, the old master tries one time too often to fool the batter in the way he did before; and frequently the untried kid comes in and gets them out the same way he did in the minors—fastball, curve, curve, fastball . . . He doesn't know any better—yet. But if he is to be around major league baseball for very long, he had better find out.

Few of the 53,000 fans who saw it at Busch Stadium in St. Louis, or of the 40 million who saw it on television, were aware of the intense drama of one of the most interesting confrontations involving decision-making in recent baseball history, in October of 1982. It came in the sixth inning of the seventh game of the World Series between the St. Louis Cardinals and Milwaukee Brewers, with the Cards down 3–1.

Pete Vuckovich, having already been voted the American League Cy Young Award for 1982, was pitching for Milwaukee with only three days rest. In the chill night air he strained his arm and ran out of steam in the sixth inning. After getting the first out with a routine grounder, he gave up a line-drive single and a double to the two Smiths of St. Louis, Ozzie and Lonnie. Looking at runners at second and third, and over to the Milwaukee bullpen where the relievers were throwing quickly to warm up in the frigid air, Pete did what he had to do. He called time out and kneeled behind the mound, not in supplication, but to unlace and remove his left shoe, shake it, smooth his sock, put it back on and relace the shoe. The second-base and third-base umpires joined the infielders to watch as he did the same with his right shoe. They watched; that was all they did. The Cardinal bench did not join their fans in the hoots and boos of protest over the four minutes that it took Vuke to get ready to pitch again.

Now the Brewers' manager, Harvey Kuenn, walked slowly out from the dugout to take the ball from Vuckovich and give it to his young lefthander, Bob McClure, who in five of the previous six games had pitched only four and one-half innings. Whitey Herzog countered by sending up veteran Gene Tenace, a righthand batter more likely than Ken Oberkfell, the lefthander, to come through with the long ball.

With confidence in McClure's control, the Milwaukee decision, after considering the intentional walk, was to pitch to Gene, but to give him nothing good to hit. A consideration in this decision was that it would give McClure a few extra hard warm-up pitches, and afford him (and them) a chance to see what action his pitches took in the dense air.

McClure fished for Tenace with fastballs up and curveballs down and in, but the old pro, who had drawn an important run-batted-in walk in a previous game, spurned the bait, and walked to load the bases for Keith Hernandez, the Cardinals' No. 3 batter, a lefthander who had been hitting southpaw pitching as successfully as right-handed. Although luckless in the first four games, Keith had begun spraying hard shots over and through the infield thereafter, and had contributed mightily to the victories that had evened the series for St. Louis at three games each. Meanwhile Mike Ramsey, a versatile utility infielder with good wheels, went in to run for Tenace, and would replace Oberkfell at third.

There was a Sophoclean inevitability to the confrontation between Bob McClure and Keith Hernandez. As boys, they had been companions of the diamond in the San Francisco area. They had played together in the Little League, Pony League, and Colt League. They had maintained their friendship while going on different paths upward through the minors to their present status as secure major league ballplayers.

As Keith had become a killer of lefthanded pitching, so Bob had become a killer of lefthanded batting. With his crossfire fastball, whipped out from behind his back with a deceptive body turn, and with a quick slider and a good curve that came in on lefthanders and broke away, and a slower curve that sank—and with Keith batting only .250 in the series and with Rollie Fingers, the Brewers' ace reliever, out with a sore arm—there was no doubt in any knowledgeable mind that in going with Bob as their best hope of getting out of their predicament, the Brewers had made the best possible choice.

Facing his friend—and with admiration for and knowledge of McClure's assortment of action pitches—Keith was more confident of being able to come through now than he would have been against Vuckovich. "I was glad when they pulled Vuke," he said after the game. "He had been throwing nasty . . . had me befuddled. Besides, I hit lefthanders pretty good. I wasn't nervous up there against Bob. I'm a disciplined hitter. I'm a better hitter with men on base. I hit third because I drive 'em in. You gotta be an animal up there, a tiger. See the ball, hit the ball. 'If I strike out, I strike out.' I was thinking base hit. A sacrifice fly doesn't do us any good. We're still a run behind with two outs."

McClure's first pitch was a crossfire inside fastball. Ball one. His second, inside, too, was a dandy slider that broke into the strike zone. Then he missed inside with another slider, and outside with a low curve. With a 3–1 count, he had to throw a strike. A walk would force in a run and, ominously, bring righthander George Hendrick, hitting .320, to the plate with still only one out.

"I'm thinking," Bob said later, "that Keith will be looking for a slider or curveball away." His catcher, Ted Simmons, a former Cardinal teammate of Hernandez, called for him to pitch what Keith would not be looking for. Ted signaled for an inside fastball, and Bob nodded agreement.

But Keith was following the convolutions of their decision. "It's three and one, and he's thinking strike. If he throws a breaking ball, he's got to come down the middle. So I'm thinking he's thinking fastball." Keith got it, and he slammed a liner into centerfield that scored the tying runs. Then George Hendrick drove in Mike Ramsey with the go-ahead run, and Bruce Sutter's split-finger fastball down and his unexpected fastball up evaded the Brewers' bats, to save the game and win the World Series for St. Louis.

"After the game," said Bob McClure, "I congratulated Keith, but I didn't say anything about how he could do this to an old buddy. Maybe I'll write him a letter."

Keith Hernandez guessing it would be old number one that he would get, and getting it. Getting the fastball because he should have gotten it—should have because Bob McClure was thinking that since number one was so clearly in order, his old buddy would therefore be expecting number two in its stead. So if he threw Hernandez the fastball he ought to have been expecting, Keith wouldn't really be expecting it! So it was fastball, slider, slider, curve, fastball—in and out, down and up, the flash of the bat, the ball streaking toward centerfield: the rhythms of the game, broken and reasserted, that Candy Cummings's curveball had made possible, back long ago.

As goes the curve, so goes baseball. King Carl Hubbell fanning Ruth, Gehrig, Foxx, Simmons, and Cronin in succession in the 1934 All-Star game. Silent Steve Carlton's slider mowing down the Los Angeles Dodgers in the 1983 National League playoffs. Don Sutton's "tailing fastball" with the mysteriously applied scuffmarks.

"Get out my work clothes, Mom. They've started to throw curveballs."

Oh, the joys and miseries they have caused while making the game of baseball our national pastime.

Mike Flanagan, 1979 Cy Young Award winner for the Baltimore Orioles, does not use either a scuffball or his "pretty good bullpen spitter" during a game, he declares. Note the four-fingered grip. *Richard Pilling*

He did it! Dave Righetti of the Yankees after he delivered a third strike to the Red Sox' Wade Boggs, giving him a no-hitter, July 4, 1983. *United Press International*

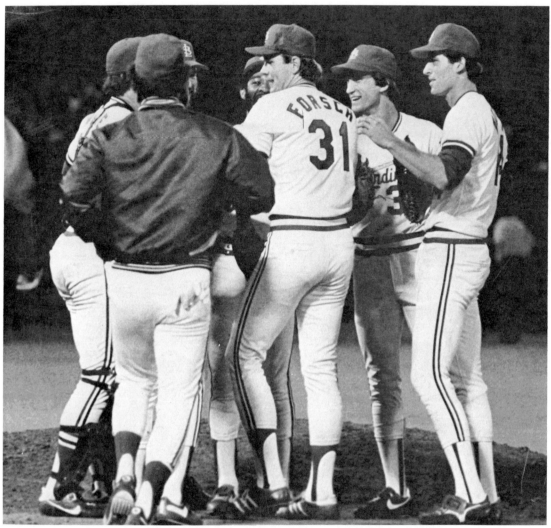

Bob Forsch's St. Louis teammates congratulate him after the veteran righthander's second no-hit game of his career, against the Montreal Expos, September 26, 1983. *The Sporting News*

INDEX